Access to History

General Editor: Keith Randell

22-12-97

The Wars of the Roses and the Yorkist Kings

John Warren

Hodder & Stoughton

A MEMBER OF T

The cover illustration shows *The Bastard of Fauconberg's attack on London, 1471* (Courtesy of University Library, Ghent).

Some other titles in the series:

Henry VII   ISBN 0 340 53880 1
Caroline Rogers

Henry VIII and the Reformation in England   ISBN 0 340 57805 X
Keith Randell

Henry VIII and the Government of England   ISBN 0 340 55352 1
Keith Randell

Edward VI and Mary: A Mid-Tudor Crisis?   ISBN 0 340 53560 1
Nigel Heard

Elizabeth I and the Government of England   ISBN 0 340 56547 0
Keith Randell

Elizabeth I: Religion and Foreign Affairs   ISBN 0 340 55518 1
John Warren

British Library Cataloguing in Publication Data

A catalogue for this is available
from the British Library

ISBN 0-340-61114-6

First published 1995

Impression number   10 9 8 7 6 5 4 3 2
Year   1999 1998 1997 1996

Typeset by Sempringham publishing services, Bedford
Printed in Great Britain for Hodder & Stoughton Educational,
a division of Hodder Headline Plc, 338 Euston Road, London NW1 3BH
by Redwood Books, Trowbridge, Wiltshire

Contents

Preface

To the general reader

Although the *Access to History* series has been designed with the needs of students studying the subject at higher examination levels very much in mind, it also has a great deal to offer the general reader. The main body of the text (i.e. ignoring the Study Guides at the ends of chapters) forms a readable and yet stimulating survey of a coherent topic as studied by historians. However, each author's aim has not merely been to provide a clear explanation of what happened in the past (to interest and inform): it has also been assumed that most readers wish to be stimulated into thinking further about the topic and to form opinions of their own about the significance of the events that are described and discussed (to be challenged). Thus, although no prior knowledge of the topic is expected on the reader's part, she or he is treated as an intelligent and thinking person throughout. The author tends to share ideas and possibilities with the reader, rather than passing on numbers of so-called 'historical truths'.

To the student reader

There are many ways in which the series can be used by students studying History at a higher level. It will, therefore, be worthwhile thinking about your own study strategy before you start your work on this book. Obviously, your strategy will vary depending on the aim you have in mind, and the time for study that is available to you.

If, for example, you want to acquire a general overview of the topic in the shortest possible time, the following approach will probably be the most effective:

1 Read Chapter 1 and think about its contents.
2 Read the 'Making notes' section at the end of Chapter 2 and decide whether it is necessary for you to read this chapter.
3 If it is, read the chapter, stopping at each heading to note down the main points that have been made.
4 Repeat stage 2 (and stage 3 where appropriate) for all the other chapters.

If, however, your aim is to gain a thorough grasp of the topic, taking however much time is necessary to do so, you may benefit from carrying out the same procedure with each chapter, as follows:

1 Read the chapter as fast as you can, and preferably at one sitting.
2 Study the flow diagram at the end of the chapter, ensuring that you understand the general 'shape' of what you have just read.

3 Read the 'Making notes' section (and the 'Answering essay questions' section, if there is one) and decide what further work you need to do on the chapter. In particularly important sections of the book, this will involve reading the chapter a second time and stopping at each heading to think about (and to write a summary of) what you have just read.

4 Attempt the 'Source-based questions' section. It will sometimes be sufficient to think through your answers, but additional understanding will often be gained by forcing yourself to write them down.

When you have finished the main chapters of the book, study the 'Further Reading' section and decide what additional reading (if any) you will do on the topic.

This book has been designed to help make your studies both enjoyable and successful. If you can think of ways in which this could have been done more effectively, please write to tell me. In the meantime, I hope that you will gain greatly from your study of History.

Keith Randell

Illustration Acknowledgements

The Publishers would like to thank the following for permission to reproduce illustrations in this volume:

Cover - The Bastard of Faucomberg's attack on London, 1471, courtesy of the University Library, Ghent

National Portrait Gallery, London p. 144 (top); by courtesy of the Society of Antiquaries of London p. 144 (bottom) and p. 145.

Every effort has been made to trace and acknowledge ownership of copyright. The Publishers will be glad to make suitable arrangements with any copyright holders whom it has not been possible to contact.

CHAPTER 1

Introduction: The Wars of the Roses and the Yorkist Kings

1 'The Past is a Foreign Country'

So say historians, but to call the past a foreign country can be misleading. After all, you can visit a foreign country, but you cannot visit the past. You might try to recreate it, but it does not work. If you go to a so-called medieval banquet, you might leave with the sound of some pleasant lute-music ringing in your ears and the tang of 'mead' or 'ale' on your tongue. But if you wanted to really recreate the past - and if modern hygiene regulations would permit - you should probably also leave with a bad case of intestinal worms.

As a foreigner abroad, you can always employ a 'native' guide. Or you can learn the language. But the best you can do for a guide to the past is choose an historian, who may prove inaccurate or quarrelsome. Of course, if you are studying English history, then you may think that the language will pose few problems. Quaint, perhaps - particularly if you are studying the fifteenth or sixteenth centuries - but at least you can be pretty sure of the meaning. Not so. Take the modern English word 'presently', meaning 'soon'. In Shakespeare's play *Othello,* the unfortunate Desdemona asks Othello when he intends to murder her. 'Presently,' he replies. Now, one might think that this would at least give Desdemona a while to prepare herself, or even to try what a little persuasion might do. But the word 'presently' meant 'immediately', and time has run out for her. So, a familiarity with the words of the past may prove dangerous. Words like 'noble', 'parliament' and even 'king' have modern meanings that must be put to one side as we look at the past.

The above comments are not intended to be off-putting. Just the opposite, in fact. For many students and general readers, this book may well provide their first real acquaintance with the fifteenth century. For some, it may also be their first topic studied beyond the level of first public examinations. This is good, because the present writer believes that part of the fascination of this period lies in its differences from the modern world. It is a challenge - an exploration, perhaps, rather than a visit to the past.

2 Blood and Gore

It is very easy to write a brief overview of the period covered by this book (c.1399-1497) and to make it sound like the ravings of an addict of melodrama. We have a thorough-going hero of a king of the House of Lancaster (Henry V) who crowns his massive military achievements against the odds by dying young (always a good way of cementing a

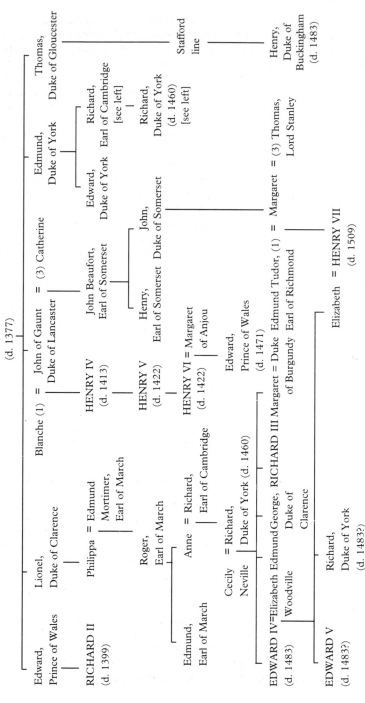

Simplified genealogical table - Lancastrians and Yorkists

growing reputation). His baby son (Henry VI), carefully schooled to kingship, repays the care of his protectors with ill-timed bouts of insanity when he ascends the throne. He loses the throne (twice) and his son and heir is killed on the battlefield. The throne is taken by Edward IV (of the House of York), whose capacity for wine, women and song (particularly women) leads him into an unfortunate marriage which sparks off rebellions and sows the seeds of future disaster. After his death, Edward's young sons are taken into the loving care of his ever-loyal younger brother (later Richard III) who honours his brother's memory by declaring Edward to be illegitimate, his sons likewise, and then (allegedly) contrives to have his nephews murdered. Richard III subsequently meets a spectacular death on the battlefield deserted by everyone (including his horse). Henry Tudor takes the throne as Henry VII, artfully smooths over the past divisions of the families of York and Lancaster by marrying Elizabeth, the daughter of Edward IV, and founds the Tudor dynasty. And the symbol of that dynasty was the Tudor rose: the blending of the red rose of Lancaster with the white rose of York.

Oddly enough, this rather torrid picture of the period known as the Wars of the Roses would not be unfamiliar to the well-read subjects of the most famous monarchs of that Tudor dynasty - Henry VIII and Elizabeth I. It served the needs of the Tudors to pay historians to present a grim picture of the doings of their predecessors. After all, would this not make their own reigns seem the more stable, the more peaceful, and the more to be valued by way of contrast?

Modern historians are, of course, more fortunate. They are not paid by monarchs to glorify their achievements and to denigrate their opponents. Nor do they see history as a method of moral and political teaching by example, as Tudor historians did. Their concerns are different, and are reflected in the content of this book.

3 Historians, Historiography and the Wars of the Roses

No detailed study of the Wars of the Roses can ignore or neglect to discuss the varying interpretations of historians, ancient and modern - the historiography (writings on history) of the period. What issues, then, have interested historians about the time known as the Wars of the Roses? First, there has been the use of the phrase 'Wars of the Roses' itself. The value of the phrase has been attacked for two reasons. In the first place, it has been argued that it ought to be discarded because it was unknown at the time of the conflicts: the warring parties - based loosely around the dynasties of Lancaster and York - did not use the red and white roses as their emblems or badges. This view can, perhaps, be itself discarded. It is true that the warring parties used a number of badges, and that the roses were by no means the most important. For example, Henry VI preferred an antelope, and Richard III a white boar. But it is

ie that the roses were recognised as symbols associated with the
ouses, and that they were used as propaganda by Henry Tudor to
claim that he had reconciled differences and brought to the weary
country a time of peace. More importantly, we are stuck with the phrase.
It is a convenient label to attach to the period, and one that has stood the
test of time.

The second objection to the 'Wars of the Roses' is more fundamental:
namely, that they were not wars at all, but scrappy, short-lived and
insignificant conflicts that scarcely merit even the name of battles. This
view, associated with a number of historians writing in the 1970s and
early 1980s, was itself an attack on the earlier and accepted view that the
Wars of the Roses were the most appalling spell in a generally appalling
and anarchic century. These so-called 'revisionist' historians were often
not content to explode what they saw as myths about the level of
violence: they were also inclined to stress the positive achievements of
the period. Compared to the rest of Europe, it seems, England was a
haven of tranquillity, where the comfortable, ill-defended homes of the
nobles and large-scale church-building programmes gave the lie to those
who argued that turmoil and terror typified the period. This issue will be
discussed in Chapter 5 of this book, but it is best to say at this stage that
the debate on the scale and impact of the Wars continues to this day.
Those historians who claimed that the effects of the Wars were much
more limited than had traditionally been thought did not go
unchallenged even in the 1970s and 1980s, and it is now clear that there
is sufficient evidence to suggest that it is just as possible to underestimate
as it is to overestimate the extent of disruption and destruction. Perhaps
we should accept that it is safe, as well as necessary, to use the phrase
'Wars of the Roses'.

It has to be recognised that, in the study of this period as in history as
a whole, certainty is virtually impossible to achieve. The evidence is, to
say the least, patchy. We have the writing of contemporary chroniclers,
but they, as the historian Antonia Gransden has suggested, often
'changed sides with remarkable facility'. In fact, what we also see is a
significant growth in the number of officially sponsored or propaganda-
style histories. *The Historie of the Arrivall of King Edward IV* is a good
example of this type of production. It provides a totally partisan account
of the successes and virtues of that Yorkist king. In addition, we have
some collections of letters. But, of course, we cannot assume, for
example, that the whole of England was little different to the troubled
East Anglia as described in the writings of the Paston family.

To complicate matters further, it is not even a simple matter to decide
when the Wars of the Roses actually took place. Perhaps the most
common view (and that adopted by this book) is that they lasted roughly
from the mid 1450s to 1487 (or 1497, when the very last blow fell). On
the other hand, it has been argued that the Wars lasted over 80 years:
from 1399 to 1485. The case goes something like this. In 1399, Richard

II was deposed by the Lancastrian Henry IV. This was a crime against God and man which brought down upon the unfortunate country a terrible civil war. The bitter rivalry between Yorkist and Lancastrian claimants was resolved only when Henry Tudor overcame Richard III at Bosworth field in 1485. It is not surprising that this interpretation has its origin in the reign of Henry Tudor. Its most eloquent and persuasive champion was Shakespeare. In his play *Henry V*, the king prays before the great battle of Agincourt:

> O God of battles! steel my soldiers' hearts;
> Possess them not with fear ...
> Not to-day, O Lord!
> O! not to-day, think not upon the fault
> My father made in compassing the crown.
> I Richard's body have interr'd anew,
> And on it have bestow'd more contrite tears
> Than from it issu'd forced drops of blood.

In Shakespeare's *Henry VI, Part II*, Richard, Duke of York gives voice to his ambition. The king he refers to is Henry VI:

> Then will I raise aloft the milk-white rose
> With whose sweet smell the air shall be perfum'd,
> And in my standard bear the arms of York,
> To grapple with the house of Lancaster;
> And, force perforce, I'll make him yield the crown,
> Whose bookish rule hath pull'd fair England down.

In the play *Richard III*, the Earl of Richmond (later Henry VII) says after the death of Richard:

> We will unite the white rose and the red:
> Smile, heaven, upon this fair conjunction ...
> England hath long been mad, and scarr'd herself;
> The brother blindly shed the brother's blood,
> The father rashly slaughter'd his own son,
> The son, compell'd, been butcher to the sire:
> All this divided York and Lancaster ...
> Now civil wounds are stopp'd, peace lives again:
> That she may long live here, God say amen!

Modern historians are less willing than their sixteenth-century predecessors to accept the judgement of God as a meaningful cause of a major conflict. Few believe that long-lasting rivalries between York and Lancaster - based upon the original usurpation of the crown by Henry IV - can be seen as causes of the Wars of the Roses. Chapters 3 and 4 focus on the causes. Two chapters have been devoted to this vital issue on the grounds that the Wars must not be seen as one set of conflicts with the same set of causes. It, therefore, makes sense to split up our discussion in this manner.

Historians are inclined to squabble over a list of causes and the relative importance to attach to them. Is it true, for example, that the most important causes reflect strain and stress within the fabric of society? In other words, were relations between classes or groups in the fifteenth century so flawed that war was a likely outcome? Or are we to look to personalities and specific incidents to explain the outbreak? Was, for example, the personality of Henry VI largely to blame? To discuss these issues requires an understanding of the nature of society in fifteenth-century England - a need that is met by Chapter 2.

Finally, historians have also been interested in the systems of government established by the Lancastrian, Yorkist and Tudor kings. 'Systems of government' is a convenient shorthand for the way in which the king's authority was enforced throughout the country, the method of collecting the revenue due to the crown and the provision of law and order. An analysis here not only provides insight into the effect of the wars on administration, but also helps us to trace change, continuity and development in the way the country was run. One major debate among historians has been over whether or not the period witnessed the first signs of a new style of kingship. This concept of 'New Monarchy' will be discussed in Chapter 6. The Victorian historian J.R. Green first used the phrase, and identified the first flowerings of New Monarchy in the reign of Edward IV. Green linked it to the Wars of the Roses by arguing that the kings from Edward's time had succeeded in crushing the power of the nobles but, in so doing, had increased their own power at the expense of the so-called liberties of the people. Kings, in fact, were increasingly despotic: that is, they ruled like tyrants, consulting nothing but their own will. This thesis was significantly amended in the early twentieth century by, among others, A.F. Pollard. Pollard argued that New Monarchy was a characteristic of the Tudors. This led to the claim that 1485, when Henry VII defeated Richard III, was a major turning-point in the history of England. It was very tempting for some historians to argue that the birth of the modern nation-state could be traced to the impact of New Monarchy. In particular, Henry VII's son, Henry VIII, in rejecting the authority of the Pope over the English Church and assuming it himself, testified to the increasing prestige and power of the monarchy. What Pollard himself disliked about Green's view of New Monarchy was its assertion that the new monarchs had little time for Parliament. Pollard admired the Tudors, and he admired the trappings of the British democratic system as well. So, he ended up with the frankly unlikely argument that Henry VIII was committed to increasing the authority of Parliament.

The 'New Monarchy' theory as a whole received a considerable buffet from G.R. Elton, writing in the 1950s. Elton accepted that

England underwent a massive transformation - a modernisation - between the first and last of the Tudors (Henry VII to Elizabeth I). But he refused to accept that monarchs, new or otherwise, were responsible. Instead, he argued that Thomas Cromwell, the far-sighted statesman and Henry VIII's chief minister, had evolved a blueprint for replacing the archaic systems of medieval government with new instruments of government organised on modern lines. The old, disunited, fragmented country, with its many local rivalries and its over-mighty nobles, was being transformed into a centralised state through the vision of one man. This argument, always controversial, has been subjected to bruising attack. Cromwell has been re-interpreted, removed from his bureaucratic offices and replaced into the back-stabbing, clique-ridden corridors of the Tudor court. He now seems much more like a man of his times than a radical innovator and his reforms more like reaction to events than visionary genius.

Nevertheless, since historians do identify significant changes in the power of the state as having occurred by Elizabeth I's reign, they also have to account for them. One possible explanation would be the impact of the Wars of the Roses. To study the Tudors without studying the Wars of the Roses would be like discussing the rise of Hitler without considering the First World War.

And finally, to give shape to the period of the Wars of the Roses, it makes sense to provide, as background to the later chapters of this book, a summary of the major political events to cover the period from 1399 to 1603: from the deposition of Richard II to the death of the last of the Tudor monarchs, Elizabeth I.

4 A Summary of Events, 1399-1603

a) The Deposition of Richard II and the Accession of Henry IV

On 22 September 1399, Henry Bolingbroke, son of John of Gaunt, Duke of Lancaster, claimed the throne of England after the deposition of Richard II, whose reign had been marked by his constant overriding of law and the property rights of his nobility - itself sufficient to stimulate the opposition that led to Richard's downfall. The simplified genealogical table on page 2 shows why the new king, Henry IV, had felt the need to declare his title to the throne in rather vague terms. If one accepted the legality of the deposition (and it was doubtful at best), then Henry's claim rested on being the *heir male* - being the person having the best claim to the throne through the male line, which stretched back to John of Gaunt, the fourth son of Edward III. However, it could be argued that the stronger claim was that of the *heir general*, whose descent was through the female line via Philippa, daughter of Lionel, Duke of Clarence, the second son of Edward III. In 1399 the *heir general* was

Philippa's grandson, Edmund, Earl of March, but he was a child and no fit opponent for Henry of Lancaster. But this claim through the Mortimer family did not go away. In particular, Richard, Duke of York, the son of Anne Mortimer, inherited that claim after the death of his uncle Edmund Mortimer in 1425. This is the origin of the so-called Yorkist title to the throne.

Henry IV rarely had the opportunity to enjoy his kingdom. He was faced with rebellions in Wales, complaints from Parliament about extravagance, more rebellions from the powerful northern nobles, the Percys, incursions from Scotland, attacks on the south coast by the French, and chronic ill-health in his later years. It is small wonder that some contemporaries were inclined to blame the king's troubles on divine retribution for his usurpation.

b) Henry V

Any doubts about the stability of the new Lancastrian dynasty were quelled by the accession of Henry V in 1413. Admittedly, there was a Yorkist plot in 1415 which aimed to put Edward Mortimer on the throne, but Mortimer himself tipped off the king. Make no mistake, Henry V was impressive. He seemed to have every quality expected of a monarch. Profiting from the internal divisions in France, he won a famous victory at Agincourt in 1415, conquered half of France, married Catherine, daughter of the French king, was acknowledged as King of France by his ally the Duke of Burgundy, and became regent and heir to the French king, Charles VI. And, despite his absences, he maintained the fullness of royal authority over the administration of England. The royal lieutenant in England, assisted and advised by a council, never presumed to initiate policy without Henry's full knowledge and support.

c) Henry VI and the Outbreak of the Wars of the Roses

Henry V died of dysentery in 1422. He was only 34 years old, and left as his heir a baby son of 9 months. However, this calamity signalled neither a wave of plots against the Lancastrians nor the collapse of government. There were certainly problems: most notably, the resentment of Henry V's youngest brother, Humphrey, Duke of Gloucester, who objected to the way in which the late king's instructions in his will had been set aside by the lords assembled in Parliament. It seems that Henry V had intended Humphrey to act more or less as regent in England until Henry VI came of age, but the lords were not prepared to accept this, preferring rule in England by a council of 17, with Gloucester as 'Protector', but without the power to make policy decisions except with council approval. Gloucester did all he could to disrupt this conciliar government in the years of Henry's minority, but, when Henry VI at last assumed the full powers of king in 1437, the council could look back on a job well done. The boy of 16 had come to power, and royal authority had not been damaged in any way. It took Henry VI himself to do that.

The details of the disasters of Henry VI's reign will be discussed in Chapter 3. Henry V had secured loyalty and stability for his crown through his conquests in France: his son's policy of seeking peace did nothing to help the morale or sense of purpose among his commanders or soldiers in his second kingdom (France). By 1453 only Calais was left: a bitter and mocking reminder of what his father had achieved and of what Henry VI had lost. He was unable to control rivalries among his nobles, and he clumsily alienated his most powerful kinsman Richard, Duke of York. In fact, he displayed few or none of the qualities required of a king. He lapsed into insanity in the autumn of 1453. York was the only possible choice for Protector, but the birth of Henry's son in October 1453 exposed the limitations and dangers of York's position. Henry's queen, Margaret of Anjou, clearly saw York as a threat to the inheritance of her son; and York could only look forward to an uncertain future. He, therefore, decided to bid for the throne. By 1460, through battle and through a formal assertion of his right to the throne, he had achieved a curious and unworkable compromise. By the Act of Accord, he recognised Henry VI as king, but was himself recognised as Henry's heir - displacing, of course, Henry's son, Edward. What York lacked was real support from his fellow nobles. In December 1460 he was killed in a skirmish near Wakefield in Yorkshire. His son, Edward, Earl of March, headed for London, where he was proclaimed king on 4 March 1461.

d) Edward IV

Edward IV made a startling contrast to Henry VI. He clearly had the presence and military acumen expected of a king, and was rewarded with a decisive victory over the Lancastrian forces at Towton in March 1461. He also had the good fortune to capture Henry VI in person some four years later. His freedom of manoeuvre was hampered by the overweening power of his greatest ally, the grasping and ambitious Earl of Warwick. Warwick 'the Kingmaker' sought to maintain his status as the king's most important subject, and was therefore greatly perturbed by Edward's marriage to the widow Elizabeth Woodville in 1464. This was partly because Warwick was looking for a foreign match for Edward to prop up the shaky international credibility of the new regime, and partly because Warwick, as a greedy and ruthless man, knew and feared what the equally greedy and ruthless Woodvilles might do to his position. And what was worse, the Woodvilles were social climbers and 'new money': distinctly *arriviste* and *nouveau-riche*. Warwick, exploiting the dissatisfaction of Edward's brother, the Duke of Clarence, encouraged the latter to join him in taking an extraordinary decision: they switched sides. In 1470 Edward IV was forced to flee abroad as

Warwick and Clarence brought about the return and restoration of Henry VI: the so-called 'Readeption'. Within a year Edward had returned, winning massive victories at Barnet and Tewkesbury. Warwick died in battle, Prince Edward met a similar fate, and Henry VI was murdered shortly after the Tewkesbury defeat.

The remainder of Edward's reign was relatively peaceful on the surface, but the problems created by the Woodville marriage did not go away. They were compounded by Edward's over-reliance on his own ability to control the rivalries occasioned by his marriage. As he fell dangerously ill in the spring of 1483, he realised that the likely minority of his eldest son, Edward, was going to be troubled by the bitterness felt towards the Woodvilles by two of his most powerful supporters, William, Lord Hastings and his own youngest brother, Richard of Gloucester. A desperate death-bed attempt to reconcile Hastings and the Woodvilles produced fair words but nothing else. When Edward died on 9 April, Gloucester and Hastings moved rapidly. The 12-year-old Edward V was journeying to London under the protection of a Woodville escort. Gloucester wrote conciliatory letters to the queen (Elizabeth Woodville) and made arrangements to meet the young king *en route*. After liberally entertaining the accompanying Woodvilles in Northampton, he had them arrested the next day. They were despatched to one of his northern strongholds for later execution. He then accompanied the young king to London, to all intents and purposes eager to see him crowned. But Gloucester may have believed that Edward V was going to be the Woodville weapon of revenge. Brought up under Woodville influence, and clearly distressed at the disappearance of his relatives, Edward would have four years at most to wait before he held power in his own hands. And what then would be the fate of his uncle Richard?

Gloucester, it seems, had no desire to wait to find out. With the support of the soldiers of Henry Stafford, Duke of Buckingham, Gloucester set out to overawe the city of London and bid for the crown. Likely opponents were dealt with ruthlessly. Hastings could be relied upon to oppose the Woodvilles, but he could also be relied upon to support the young Edward. So he was arrested and then executed with a haste that shocked the capital. Of course, even Gloucester needed a claim of some sort to the throne, and he therefore employed a tame priest to provide the interesting and convenient information that Edward's two sons were illegitimate. For good measure, Gloucester also accused his own mother of adultery, claiming that Edward IV was not the son of Richard of York.

e) The Reign of Richard III

Richard of Gloucester was crowned on 6 July 1483. Whatever pains he took to secure the crown, including the alleged murder of the so-called

'Princes in the Tower', he had little leisure to enjoy his success. In a curious parallel with Warwick the Kingmaker, Richard's most powerful and trusted ally, the Duke of Buckingham, was involved in an unsuccessful rebellion within months of Richard's accession. And in 1484 Richard's only son, Edward, died. In August 1485, and in an atmosphere of uncertainty and suspicion, Richard sought to defend his crown in battle against a somewhat obscure pretender - Henry Tudor, Earl of Richmond. Treachery on the battlefield led to Richard's death.

f) The Reign of Henry VII

It would seem that much of the narrative of events so far has dealt with the dangers posed to the crown by 'over-mighty' nobles. Henry VII certainly faced difficulties from various pretenders to his throne, but his reign is nevertheless marked by a change in the relationship between noble and king. Henry succeeded in entangling his nobles in a financial and political web. The more they struggled, the more deeply they became entwined. His main weapon was a form of bond or contract called a recognisance. A noble would be asked - or obliged - to enter into a recognisance with the king which demanded his good behaviour. Bad behaviour might mean nothing more than failing to ensure law and order in one's own territories: by no means an easy task in a violent age. But the cost of failure was high. The fear of massive fines for the breaking of recognisances made for nervous nobles.

As for the pretenders, it is significant that they were fakes. This reveals very clearly just how few real alternatives there were to Henry Tudor, despite the relative weakness of his claim to the throne. The first and most dangerous, Lambert Simnel, claimed to be the Earl of Warwick (odd, since the latter was in the Tower of London on Henry's orders). Simnel did receive sufficient backing from the Earl of Lincoln (nephew of Richard III) to bring Henry to a tough battle at Stoke in 1487. But the second pretender, Perkin Warbeck (claiming to be the youngest son of Edward IV) was no real danger, although Henry had to be wary of foreign powers seeking to exploit such claims.

g) The Reign of Henry VIII

Unsurprisingly, there was a real sense of rejoicing when Henry VII died in 1509. His son, Henry VIII, promised to be generous where his father had been mean, open-hearted where his father had been suspicious and distrustful, and fond of the company of his nobility where his father had kept them at arm's length. Henry VII's foreign policy had been aimed at legitimising the Tudor dynasty abroad and at pursuing the relatively cheap option of peace through alliance. This was sensible and partly successful, but it was not glorious. His son, on the other hand, preferred the rôle-model of Henry V. His reign was marked by aggression towards France in the pursuit of glory. It was also marked by the more desperate pursuit of a male heir. The consequences of the search for a divorce from the ageing Catherine of Aragon are well known: the cutting of the age-old ties between the Roman Catholic Church and the English Church, the dissolution of the monasteries, and assumption by the king of the title 'Supreme Head of the Church of England'. Such policies were bound to create opposition, but it would be quite wrong to argue that the remaining members of the House of York were simply waiting in the wings, ready to leap on to the stage to proclaim their titles. It is not as if Henry VIII had seen such families as the Courtenays, Nevilles and Poles as threats from the start of his reign. They had not been deprived of his generosity, and he had employed Reginald Pole as part of his campaign to secure the approval of foreign universities for the annulment of his marriage. But, once crises and potential rebellions occurred, Henry had no intention of letting the House of York become a willing or unwilling focus for disloyalty. Courtenay, Henry Pole and Sir Edward Neville were all executed in 1538. Sons of executed fathers disappeared into the Tower. Age and sex were no defence: Margaret Pole, countess of Salisbury and ancient by any standards, was executed in 1541 after the discovery of a minor Neville plot. Reginald Pole was another matter. He was being used as the Pope's agent to collect support for rebels against Henry, although he moved too slowly to take advantage of the serious, pro-Catholic rebellion of 1536 known as the Pilgrimage of Grace. Henry unsuccessfully tried to have him kidnapped and despatched to England. But what motivated Pole was less the claims of the House of York than those of orthodox Catholicism. As Cardinal, Reginald Pole was later to become Archbishop of Canterbury to another Tudor - Mary I, Henry's eldest daughter.

h) The final three Tudors: Edward VI, Mary I and Elizabeth I.

When Henry VIII died in 1547, his only son, Edward, was just nine years old. Although this meant another minority, it was not one plagued with the infighting of Yorkist and Lancastrian as there were no surviving members of these families. Thus Edward VI's title was never in doubt, and political conflict focussed on who was to hold the Protectorship. The Duke of Somerset, Edward Seymour, was ousted by a rival, the Duke of Northumberland, not because of dynastic rivalry but because of incompetence and a failure to protect the interests of his own class. When Edward VI died in 1553 and the Catholic Mary I took the throne, opposition was religious rather than dynastic: as, indeed, it was for her Protestant successor and half-sister, Elizabeth I. The Tudor rose had, it seemed, fully assimilated both red and white: but the rose had no buds. On 24 March 1603, Elizabeth I died: and, with her, the Tudor dynasty.

Making notes on 'Introduction: *The Wars of the Roses and the Yorkist Kings'*

Making notes is an irritation, a confusion, a grinding evil, a mystery and a total necessity. Students are often asked to pick out the 'important parts', but, having just made the acquaintance of the topic, have little or no idea what these might be. To help ease the burden, the note-making sections of this book suggest where notes might be needed and offer guidance on what are the crucial issues.

Chapter 1 provides an overview of the Wars of the Roses. The notes you make under the headings suggested below can, therefore, be expected to give you no more than an outline of the main issues and events. Issues such as the causes of the Wars are, of course, covered in detail in later chapters. If, by the time you have finished your notes, you have some sense of the overall shape or feel of the topic, then you have been successful.

1   Good news - notes unnecessary.
2   Historians, historiography and the Wars of the Roses
2.1   What issues interest historians in the Wars of the Roses?
3   A summary of events
3.1   Why did some contemporaries see the problems of Henry IV's
      reign as punishment from God?
3.2   Why did Henry V acquire such a fine reputation?
3.3   How successful was the royal council during Henry VI's minority?
3.4   In outline, what are the main events from Henry VI's accession to
      the usurpation of the throne by Edward, Earl of March, in 1461?
3.5   How did the Readeption come about?
3.6   How did Edward IV recover his throne?
3.7   How did the usurpation of the throne by Richard of Gloucester
      come about?
3.8   What were the main characteristics of Richard III's reign?
3.9   What challenges faced Henry Tudor? How successfully were they
      overcome?
3.10 How significant was the Yorkist threat to Henry VII's Tudor
      successors?

CHAPTER 2

England in the Mid-Fifteenth Century

1 What was the Kingdom of England?

'Before you start to plan your essay, identify the key words in the title. Define them if you need to. Only then can you start to decide on the content and the argument of your essay.' This sort of plea rings in the ears of many a student, and good advice it is too. It is also good advice for the writer of this chapter, because there are two key words in the heading to section 1 that need defining, simple as they seem to be. These words are 'England' and 'kingdom'. Modern meanings are dangerously misleading, and it is important to get these words right. The Wars of the Roses happened in a place called the Kingdom of England, and without an understanding of what that meant, it will be impossible to understand the society that created and suffered from the conflicts.

'Kingdom' seems easy enough to define: a country ruled by a king. What was meant by the word 'king' in the fifteenth century will be discussed in section 4. As for 'England', it would be a really spectacular mistake to refer to it as Britain. The word 'Britain' was used in the fifteenth century, but it was a geographical expression - like 'the British Isles' - and not a political one. Scotland was an independent kingdom, but one with a much smaller population and with much less wealth than England. It was a mark of England's superior power that the kings of Scotland were in theory supposed to swear allegiance to the kings of England. But it was not easy for the English to translate their superiority into practice. In the first place, Scotland could and did turn to France for an alliance against England. The Hundred Years War (1337-1453) had, of course, made the Scots alliance very welcome from the French point of view. Second, the English kings did not find it easy to launch invasions of Scotland from the north of England. Their problem was that the north was remote from the king's power base in the south of England. He had no standing (permanent) army in the north (or anywhere else, for that matter) to hammer or restrain the Scots. He had to rely on the great northern noble families - especially the Percy Earls of Northumberland - to deal with them. And these border nobles jealously guarded their near-independence. Their power was buttressed by the fierce loyalty of the non-noble landowning classes (the gentry). Looking out from their fortified towers and manor houses, the northern gentry gave support to one of the Percies because it was a Percy who had the power to help them in the to-and-fro of border raiding. The king of England did not.

Wales had much in common with the north of England. Allegiance was owed to the English crown, but great nobles in the east and south of

Wales (the Marches) operated with near-regal powers. In particular, the Marcher lords held 'liberties', which meant that they, and not the king, superintended the legal system in those areas.

However, no noble or group of nobles in the north or Wales could actually challenge the power of the king or deny his ultimate authority. Faced with a rebellion against him, the king had the military power, the resources and (usually) the support to crush it completely. It was different in Ireland, where the king of England's title was 'Lord of Ireland' and no more. In fact, the king's control extended no further than an area around Dublin known as the Pale. Outside the Pale were the Anglo-Irish lords, the descendants of the Norman conquerors of Ireland. They were virtually kings in their own lands. If it suited their interests, they might offer some token of their supposed allegiance to England. Outside these lands lay the Ireland of the Gaelic chieftains, where the king's authority was completely rejected. But Ireland was certainly useful to English kings. If nothing else, it was a good place to send inconvenient, troublesome, or over-ambitious English nobles.

2 England, France and the Hundred Years War

Scotland, Ireland and the Welsh Marches were important to the medieval English king, but it was France that caused his pulse to race and his sword arm to itch. This is partly due to the French origin of the kings of England dating back to the time of the Norman conquest in 1066, and partly because they had considerable lands in France. In addition, the claims of the kings of England to the throne of France gave some kind of vaguely moral excuse for the occasional conflicts between 1337-1453 known rather grandly as the Hundred Years War. A war with France offered a diversion from troubles at home - particularly with quarrelsome nobles - but also the possibility of massive profit. The English campaigns of the first 60 or so years were simply out to cause as much damage and to seize as much booty as possible. But the wars of Henry V (1415-22) were campaigns of conquest, with the throne of France his hoped-for prize.

3 The Hundred Years War and National Identity

War against the French probably gave a boost to feelings of nationalism - of shared 'Englishness' - among the nobles of England. After all, facing an enemy across a battlefield gave them an excellent incentive to develop a sense of togetherness. It is difficult to prove it, but one piece of evidence can be produced to support the claim that nationalism was increasing. This is the change that was taking place in the status of the English language. In the early fourteenth century, French was the preferred language of the upper classes. The nobles could speak English,

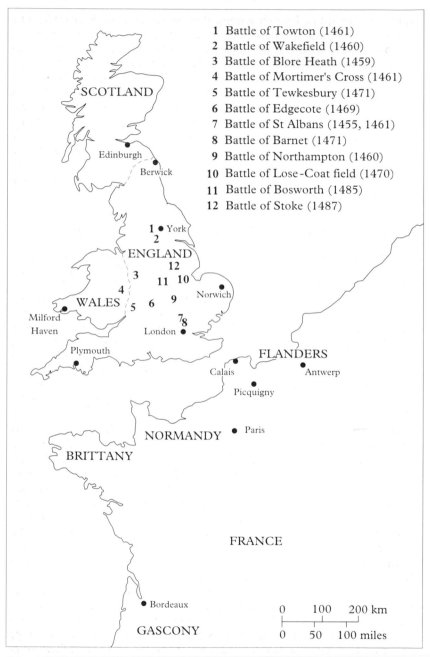

1 Battle of Towton (1461)
2 Battle of Wakefield (1460)
3 Battle of Blore Heath (1459)
4 Battle of Mortimer's Cross (1461)
5 Battle of Tewkesbury (1471)
6 Battle of Edgecote (1469)
7 Battle of St Albans (1455, 1461)
8 Battle of Barnet (1471)
9 Battle of Northampton (1460)
10 Battle of Lose-Coat field (1470)
11 Battle of Bosworth (1485)
12 Battle of Stoke (1487)

Map of England, Scotland, and France, with the main battles of the Wars of the Roses but chose to speak French among themselves as a mark of rank. The Chester monk, Ranulf Higden, commented in his *Polychronicon* (written in about 1327) that the young English nobles are taught 'to leave their own language, and to construe their lessons in French, and have been since the Normans first came into England'. Of course, Higden is complaining, and his complaint is a sign that some people, at least, were unhappy with the situation. In the 1380s, the *Polychronicon* itself was translated into English from Latin. The translator, John Trevisa, noted that 'Gentlemen have now for the most part given up teaching their children French'. As the fourteenth century went on, there was a massive flowering of literature in English for the upper classes. They clearly saw English as their language, and one that was in every way the equal of French.

4 The Structure of English Society - an Introduction

This section, together with sections 5, 6 and 7, explains in some detail the social structure of the kingdom of England. Its aim, however, is not simply to provide a description for the sake of it. This would be like writing an essay which has too much narrative irrelevant to the question. Instead, the discussion is intended to provide the reader with the background necessary to an understanding of the causes of the Wars of the Roses. If it is to be argued that some of the causes stem from the nature of society itself, then it is vital to know what society was like. The discussion will, therefore, not seek to provide a full account of every class and occupation in England. Instead, it will look more closely at the issue of power, and in this way concentrate on those aspects important to the Wars themselves.

To explain the structure of society and how it worked means answering two questions. First, what was its purpose? Second, who had how much power over whom? The first answer is simple enough, and reflected the Christian world-view. Human society had no purpose in itself except as a preparation for the Four Last Things: Death, Judgement, Heaven and Hell. It was the task of the Church to teach, persuade and threaten the Christian towards salvation. Archbishops, bishops, abbots, priests, monks and the many other servants of the Church were therefore members of the so-called 'first estate'. But mankind was sinful, and life was turbulent and violent: and so, spiritual leadership would come to nothing unless the Christian and the Church herself were protected by the power of the sword. Here lies the justification for kingship itself. The king was appointed by God as a defender of his subjects. To do this, he had to have authority over them - like the parent has over the child. A typically fifteenth-century analogy compared society as a whole to a human body. At its head was the king, and he, therefore, guided and directed that society like the head directs and guides the body. Of course, the king could not do it alone. God therefore instituted the so-called 'second estate' or aristocracy to help him. But where did this leave the ordinary people - the 'commonalty' or 'third estate'? Their rôle was different, but, in theory at least, just as important. Bodies need heads, but heads need bodies just as surely. The third estate worked in field and town to provide for the needs of the other two estates. So, the three estates were supposedly bound together in mutual interest. Conflict between them would be self-mutilation or, at worst, suicide.

The head and body analogy is well expressed by John Russell, Bishop of Lincoln, in the following extract from a draft speech of his in 1483.

1 In this body politic of England there are three estates as principal members under one head - the estate of the lords spiritual, the estate of the lords temporal, and the estate of the commonalty. The head is our sovereign lord the king ... What due proportion and
5 harmony ought to be in this body, amongst all the members, great and small, St Paul, taking his simile from the natural body of man, declares ... that, like as in the natural body there is no member, be he never so noble, that may say to the least or the vilest of them all, 'I have no need of you', but that each has his necessary and
10 appropriate work, so it is in the mystical or politic body of the congregation of the people, that every estate is ordained to support the other.

This was an immensely rigid class structure. Modern western liberal culture would regard it as quite wrong. If you believe in ideas such as 'equality of opportunity' and the 'classless society', then you would find it distasteful to restrict a person's chance of getting on in the world just because he or she happened to be born in a certain class. But this kind of attitude would make no sense to the medieval mind. To do one's duty within one's allotted estate was the key to salvation. Ambition to better oneself socially was, in theory, fighting against the decrees of God. This attitude was supported by the so-called sumptuary laws. These laid down exactly what quality of clothing was appropriate for the various estates and sub-divisions of those estates (or degrees). The sumptuary law of 1363 ordered that

Carters, ploughmen. drivers of the plough, oxherds, cowherds, shepherds ... and other people that have not forty shillings worth of goods ... shall not take or wear any manner of cloth but blanket and russe, of wool, worth not more than twelve pence.

The sumptuary law of 1463 added some fashion detail, explaining that knights and below were forbidden to wear jackets, 'but of such a length as may cover his buttocks and privy parts'.

But it has to be said that sermons and laws are one thing, reality often another. It is ironic that Russell's sermon on natural order and unity could not be given because that sitting of Parliament was disrupted by the news of a rebellion against the king. And we ought to recognise that laws are often brought in to stop offensive behaviour that already exists. This certainly seems true of the sumptuary laws. Some people, at least, had ambition to rise above their station.

There is, indeed, other evidence that the division of society into three estates was not quite so inflexible as the theory would suggest. The historian Maurice Keen has argued in his *English Society in the Later Middle Ages* that a new diversity in English society can be identified by around 1500. Keen is not suggesting that the traditional three-estates framework was being discarded. Instead, new occupations - new 'degrees' - had to be slotted in to the old system. The newly-prosperous tenant farmer class - the yeomanry - is a case in point. Keen finds an early sign of this kind of change in literary evidence, such as Geoffrey Chaucer's exuberant *Canterbury Tales*. This unfinished poem of the 1380s describes in its General Prologue a cross-section of English society: a group of pilgrims on the way to the shrine of St Thomas Becket in Canterbury. Chaucer apologises for not putting his pilgrims into the correct descending order of social importance. However, there are a number described who do not fit readily into the standard system. Where does a man of law, a merchant, or a franklin (a minor landowner) fit into the three estates? In any case, Chaucer himself was a rising man. The son of a wine-merchant, he married into the aristocracy and pursued a career in the royal service as a diplomat and controller of customs in the port of London.

This is not to suggest that peasants ever became earls! The shifts in social structure were much more subtle than that. The divisions of society were not breaking down. If they were, then it might be argued that the Wars of the Roses were class wars - struggles between estates for dominance. But there is no real possibility of seeing the Wars of the Roses as a conflict of this type. The changes we have identified would not cause revolution, though they might create resentment in individual cases. That resentment might come from the offended pride of the aristocracy. The second estate was obsessed with pride of birth. Pedigree, ancestry, lineage: all these were to be researched, praised and defended against social climbers. A noble might well wish to defend his outraged sense of family honour against the very occasional merchant who breached the walls of the second estate. More likely, our noble would be faced with a lesser aristocrat on the rise. This could be a cause of considerable conflict locally and even nationally if the die-hard and the newcomer belonged to opposing factions. The term 'faction', or group of people who worked together for political gain, will indeed become more than familiar as we study the causes of the Wars of the Roses in later chapters.

5 The Rôle of the King

This section examines three issues. We need to remind ourselves of the king's position in the social structure, to establish what his duties were, and to assess the extent of his power. To do this, there are two things we ought to bear in mind. First, it would be easy enough to paint a neat picture of a king's powers in theory. But in practice, these powers were affected by the personality of the king, his relations with his nobility and many other factors. Second, many readers will approach this section with a picture in mind of a king of the Middle Ages which is made up of images courtesy of portrait galleries and Hollywood epics. Most of these - in one way or another - emphasise the seemingly vast power of a monarch, often expressed through arbitrary decisions, gigantic over-eating, manic aggression and shrieks of 'Off with his head!'. This kind of cultural baggage is fun but not particularly helpful to our present needs. It would be as well to stow it away as we examine the issues on the rôle of the king.

The king, of course, stands outside the three estates. As Russell suggested, he was the head directing the body or, to use another metaphor, the linchpin that held together English society. In the fifteenth century it was believed that the king was placed - as was each member of the three estates - in his position by God. In the king's case this belief was vividly represented through the symbols of the coronation rituals. The king was anointed with holy oil as a sign of God's grace. The oil used in Henry VI's coronation was supposedly given by the Virgin Mary, mother of Jesus, to the Archbishop of Canterbury and future martyr Thomas Becket. The oil was left on the king's head and body for eight days and was then washed off. A little tepid white wine, it seems, cleaned it all away nicely. On occasions, the effect of the oil was more than symbolic. The story goes that Henry IV acquired a bumper crop of lice on the royal head.

Although the king could not claim the priestly powers of saying Mass or offering forgiveness for sins, the coronation ceremonies raised him above ordinary men. To seek to overthrow an anointed king was a sin against God. This did not mean that rebellion never happened, but that it generally did not take the form of an attempt to depose the king. Even on the rare occasions where this was the intention, conspirators would announce that their aim was to free the king from his evil advisers. The point is that incompetence on the part of a king was no excuse for deposition. He inherited a throne by virtue of royal blood, not through passing an interview panel. There was no period of probation for a king.

One vital question concerns the amount of power the king had. Did the God-given, sacred character of kingship mean that the king had absolute power? In other words, did he rule without needing to consider the wishes of those he governed? The short answer is, 'no'. Over the years there had developed some defences against a tyrannical monarch.

In particular, the king could not make, scrap or rule without laws. Nor could he suddenly take it into his head to demand with menaces a tax from his subjects. For laws and for taxes, he was obliged to get the agreement of a parliament. This is clearly stated in a work, *De Laudibus Legum Angliae* (In praise of the Laws of England), written in the early 1470s by Sir John Fortescue, Lord Chief Justice under Henry VI.

> 1 The king cannot at his pleasure change the laws of his kingdom ...
>   the statutes of England are established not only by the prince's will
>   but by the assent of the whole kingdom ... the king of England does
>   not by himself or his ministers impose on his subject any tallage [a
> 5 tax imposed without consultation] or burden, nor change their
>   laws nor make new ones, without the express consent or
>   concession of his whole kingdom in his parliament.

However, a king's independent rights and privileges - his prerogatives - remained considerable. Parliament itself sat as and when he called it. He was by far the kingdom's greatest landowner, and land meant wealth and power. From this came the king's patronage. In other words, he could use crown lands and his other sources of income to offer tasty rewards for service and loyalty.

War was the king's to decide and declare. His subjects were expected to give him the necessary military support in defence of his interests at home or abroad. 'His interests', note - not theirs. The kingdom was, in theory, the king's personal property, to do with as he wished. But in practice, of course, the actions of a king affected too many people for him to be totally irresponsible or utterly heedless of the interests of others in war and diplomacy.

So far, then, it has been established that the king was indeed seen as God's appointee. But he was appointed for a purpose: the defence of the realm and his people. No-one disputed that monarchy was necessary. No-one disputed that a king should be powerful. No-one suggested that kings could be chosen by the people on the basis of their likely success in meeting the challenge. But this did not mean that the king had unlimited power, or that his actions were viewed uncritically. Nor does it mean that the king was expected to rule unaided. The following sections examine the relations between king and his most important subjects and with his agencies of government, such as the royal council and parliament. As we do this bear in mind two questions:

(i) Where did power lie?
(ii) What qualities did a king need to be an effective ruler?

6 The Nobility: a Definition

Any term used to describe a class of people is bound to be vague. The widest, and perhaps most useful, definition of a noble would be anyone whose wealth came primarily from ownership of land. But there are, of course, important gradations within the rank itself. At the top we have the greater nobility or peerage: perhaps some 50 or 60 in number, defined by summons to the Lords at the calling of a Parliament. The *crème de la crème* of these nobles would be those with some family relationship to the king and/or particularly large landed estates. A neutral term for these powerful men would be 'magnate'. A less neutral term would be 'over-mighty subject', although this might perhaps say as much about the king and his relationships with the magnates as it would about the magnates themselves.

The lesser nobility may be termed the 'gentry'. The historian Lander has estimated that they would make up between 2 and 2.5 per cent of the population. A member of the gentry might be referred to as 'esquire' or 'gentleman'; on the other hand, he might have advanced to knighthood.

7 The Nobility and the King

It is absolutely essential to appreciate that it was on the relationship between the king and his nobility that the security and stability of England depended. We recall that the fundamental task of the king was to defend Church and country. The king had no civil service in any meaningful sense, no police force and no local authority through which he could provide law and order. He therefore relied upon his nobility. The source of the power of both king and nobility was ownership of land. In a violent age, that power had to be translated into armed force if the need arose. The system that defined the relationship between king, nobility and armed power is known as feudalism.

a) Feudalism

The bond between king and nobility was essentially a legal one - the so-called 'feudal contract'. What is offered here is a very brief and perhaps simplistic description of the essence of feudalism. The feudal contract rested on the assumption that the entire country belonged to the king. The king kept in his own control substantial crown lands, but offered to his chief supporters (the magnates) lands which they held as tenants-in-chief. In return, they had to be prepared to provide a specified number and type of men-at-arms for the king whenever he needed them. The king could demand a payment known as a 'relief' when a tenant-in-chief died and his heir inherited the lands (or 'fief'). The king also had rights of wardship. If a tenant-in-chief died and the heir was a minor (i.e. too young to take up the father's place), then the lands were administered by the king. Alternatively, the right to administer them could be sold to the highest bidder. 'Administer' in this context might well mean 'exploit'. A noble with rights of wardship might use them to marry the ward into his own family. This was a very convenient way of building up one's lands and power.

The tenants-in-chief could operate almost exactly the same system, with very similar rights. In this way, they offered parts of the land given them by the king to members of the lesser nobility. Technically, this was called 'retaining'. The person who took the land was a 'retainer' and a group of such retainers a 'retinue'. The contract itself was called an 'indenture' (because the written contract was folded and then divided across an indented line, each party keeping one half of it).

However, it is vital to note that, by the fifteenth century, the feudal system had undergone significant changes. The phrase 'tenants-in-chief' implies that the king was purely renting land to his magnates. However, some time before 1400 it became established that those lands were regarded in law as the property of the magnate and not of the king. They could be defended in the courts against the king. They returned to the king only if a magnate were found guilty of treason. In this case, Parliament would, at the king's request, pass an act of attainder to declare lands forfeit. Similarly, when the magnate offered land to a retainer, then that land was offered as hereditary freehold and not to rent. But the feudal 'incidents' or rights of wardship and relief remained. Although these developments were important, perhaps the most significant change in the nature of feudalism was what is known to historians as 'Bastard feudalism'.

b) Bastard Feudalism

'Bastard feudalism' is a term used to describe an increasing readiness among the nobility to offer and to accept money instead of land when entering into the feudal contract. The indenture might demand the usual military support from retainers (particularly in the remoter and more troubled areas of the north and Wales), but it was also used to secure the services of administrators and lawyers. For a magnate, retaining by, say, an annual fee had its distinct advantages. By offering money instead of land he could afford to keep more retainers. Retaining by offering money enabled him to expand his network of influence among the local gentry and build up his following (or 'affinity', to use the contemporary term). In return for becoming retainers, the gentry would expect to rely upon the 'good lordship' of the magnate. This would help them in quarrels, legal and otherwise. A retainer who fell foul of the law might well expect his lord to use his influence to make sure that the verdict in a court case favoured the retainer. This practice was known as 'maintenance' (see page 36). The magnate might offer his retainer his 'livery' - a badge or uniform that showed to all concerned who was with whom. This might also be useful in the courtroom (see page 36).

It has been alleged that bastard feudalism created instability, injustice and over-mighty magnates. In this way, it might be seen as a cause of the Wars of the Roses. Perhaps so, perhaps not. This issue is discussed in Chapter 3. At this stage, there are two things we might bear in mind. First, bastard feudalism was not an invention of the period immediately before the Wars of the Roses. It can be identified as being firmly established in the fourteenth century. Second, a weak king was often one who found it difficult to control his nobility. The rivalries of magnates might spill over into armed confrontations, and the system of justice would often be perverted by the sword. If, therefore, bastard feudalism did give the great nobles more power, then a weak king would be even weaker as a result.

8) The Church

To speak of the fifteenth-century Church of England is quite wrong. There was no such body. The Church in England, however, is a different matter. The distinction is simple: the English Church was part of the Catholic ('universal') church, whose head was the Pope in Rome. Given that the purpose of society was to fulfil God's will and to enable Christian people to win salvation, it is hardly surprising that the Pope's theoretical powers were vast. In fact, he claimed supreme authority over the whole of Christian society. This claim rested on the words of Christ to St Peter in Matthew 16, where it appears that Peter is made the foundation stone of the Church. The powers of Peter were inherited, it was said, by successive popes - Peter being the first pope. The Church had the vital task of guiding the faithful to Heaven and away from the terrible fires of everlasting punishment in Hell. Secular society, and those in authority over it, were therefore servants of the Church. The fundamental purpose of those wielding secular power was, as we have seen, to defend the Church. Strictly speaking, then, the Pope had the right to direct - or even to depose - any king.

Very few indeed denied that the Pope was the spiritual leader of Christendom, or that his pronouncements on Church teaching (doctrine) were to be obeyed. An attack on these powers was an attack of the unity of the Church. However, medieval European kings found it difficult to accept that the Church in their countries, as a massive and powerful institution - a great landowner, and one whose many powers constantly affected secular society - should remain completely outside their control. The Middle Ages saw vicious struggles for control of the Church between Pope and king. What were the issues? The 'liberty of the Church' was, perhaps, the most fundamental one. Was king or Pope to select bishops and abbots? Were those in the employ of the Church who committed crimes to be punished by the Church or by the king?

By the fifteenth century, there is little doubt that the kings of England had got the upper hand. There was legislation (the Statute of Provisors, 1390) which could be used to prevent the Pope from appointing whom he wished to the important Church positions. Also, the Statute of Praemunire (1393) could bring the force of law against anyone who attempted to appeal to the Pope on anything which might 'touch the king our lord, against him, his crown or his regality or his realm'.

Kings were not, in fact, claiming the right to appoint bishops - just to choose them. There is a difference. The fundamentally spiritual act of appointing a churchman was a job for the Church. The Pope alone could create a bishop or move him from one see (bishopric) to another. But it was also understood that the Pope should never refuse the candidate chosen by the king. Because the senior clergy were of great value to the king as royal administrators, it was vital to him that the right men were appointed.

9 The Cities, Towns and Trade

If twentieth-century Britain is largely dominated by towns and cities, the same cannot be said of fifteenth-century England. At that time, roughly nine-tenths of the population of England lived in rural areas. For them, life revolved around the cycle of the seasons and the harvesting of the crops. A villager's experience was limited by the borders of his parish. Unless a person travelled about on business (like a merchant) or had the money and leisure to make visits for pleasure (like the gentry), he rarely left the small community that made up the village itself. Strangers were spotted instantly and greeted with suspicion.

By modern standards, the fifteenth-century town or city was tiny. London itself had roughly 45,000 inhabitants, and was by far the largest of the English cities, as well as the only one to compare with the great cities of continental Europe. It owed its unique position to three factors. First, it was the usual residence of the royal court and therefore the country's political capital. Second, it was the largest port in the country and dominated the export trade in cloth. Third, it was the home of the wealthiest merchants. Norwich, probably the second biggest city, had a population of not much more than 10,000. Nine others, including York and Bristol, had populations of over 6,000. For most towns, the fifteenth century was a period of decay and decreasing population, in part through the ravages of bubonic plague. The vast majority of towns served as little more than markets for the surrounding countryside. However, the towns and cities involved in textile manufacture were not just serving the domestic market. From the mid-thirteenth century onwards, England dominated the European market for woollen cloth. However, this did not translate into great increases in the size and influence of cities (with the exception of London). In fact, almost the opposite was the case. The demand for cloth encouraged competition from smaller country towns in such areas as the West Riding of Yorkshire and the Cotswolds. They were more conveniently situated near the raw material (wool) and the power-source useful for parts of the manufacturing process (swift-flowing streams for water-wheels). Rents in such towns were lower than in their larger competitors, and merchants there did not face the often extravagant demands on their time and purse involved in assuming civic office in a city like Bristol or Norwich. There is, in fact, evidence that it was increasingly difficult in the fifteenth century to find citizens willing to support the burdens of such offices.

There are three important issues for us to consider in the context of the major themes of this book. First, to what extent did the larger towns and their governing élites of wealthy men possess political muscle on a national scale? Did they rival the great noble landowners? The short answer is that they did not. The undeniable wealth of a great merchant simply did not translate into an armed retinue. Wealth based on commerce is one thing, wealth based on land and the feudal system quite another. Commerce and armed conflict are uneasy bedfellows. This is why even the great merchants of London avoided taking part in the quarrels of magnates. If possible, they would try to keep the city neutral in any major armed conflict within the kingdom. Of course, the strategic importance, prestige and the wealth of London meant that it would inevitably be the target of political factions: maintaining such neutrality was unlikely to be easy. But, as we shall see in Chapter 5, the city authorities certainly tried. If the armies of the magnates could be kept out of London, then so much the better.

The second issue concerns the impact of the Wars of the Roses on towns and trade. This will be discussed in Chapter 5 as one important element within the broader analysis of the impact of the Wars on English society as a whole.

Finally, the policies of the Yorkist kings towards towns and trade will be discussed in Chapter 6. There are, however, general points to be made at this stage. Kings could not afford to ignore towns. After all, they were expected to interest themselves in the well-being of all their subjects. Economic self-interest also played its part. Neither kings nor magnates were averse to engaging in trading ventures themselves. Merchants were undeniably useful in lending money to kings, and their willingness or otherwise so to do can be taken as a rough barometer of the confidence inspired by a king's government. Also, a thriving import and export trade increased the wealth of the king through his receipts from customs dues. Towns elected members of the Commons, and the Commons provided taxes. However, it has to be said that the world-view of the late medieval king was closer to that of the aristocracy than to that of the urban élites. The king could identify with the tastes, needs and value-systems of the landed military aristocracy: his captains of industry and commerce were worthy, but their concerns were not those of the hunting field, the glory of war and the pride of lineage. We must not, therefore, expect a king to favour the interests of the merchant classes above those of his aristocracy, or to pursue well thought-out and consistent economic policies. Foreign trade was important, but it was never allowed to direct a king's foreign policy. If it needed to be sacrificed to a king's desire for glory or the pursuit of a particular marriage to further the security of his dynasty, then sacrificed it would be.

10 The Third Estate - the Labourers

This will be a short section, for two main reasons. First, it has to be admitted that it is far more difficult to reconstruct the world of the peasant than it is to do the same for those in the classes above. The simple reason for this is that what evidence we have generally comes from those in authority and not from the peasants themselves. Second, a book about the Wars of the Roses is inevitably going to concentrate on power and those who possessed it. By and large, the peasant did not. This is not to say that landowners ignored the very real danger of a united and rebellious peasantry, having had the Peasants' Revolt of 1381 to remind them. But it meant that no magnate was going to take the risk of arming peasants as part of a rebellion of his own.

The Black Death of the fourteenth century had resulted in massive rural (and urban) depopulation. This meant that there was more land available for peasants to rent. The other side of this coin was that the nobility experienced difficulty in getting enough peasants to work the land. The impact of this on the traditional system whereby the poorest peasants were bound to the Lord of the Manor by ties of serfdom was considerable. A serf - or 'bondsman' - had been subject to an oppressive variety of so-called manorial rights. These included the requirement to work so many days per week in the lord's fields, to make a payment to the lord on the marriage of a serf's daughter and the 'heriot', where the lord demanded a varying percentage of the property of the deceased serf. These rights were, however, difficult to enforce in a time of labour shortage, when a labourer might have the audacity to bargain for wages and conditions of service and simply leave the village if dissatisfied. Indeed, the relatively strong position of some labourers enabled them to rent considerable amounts of land (say at least 60 acres), employ men, send children to school, give charity to the poor, and become people of some status in the village and beyond. This new and prosperous class was termed 'yeomen', and it was a mark of this status that some might be called upon to serve on county juries.

Despite the development of the yeomanry, it has to be said that the prosperity among the peasantry in the fifteenth century was a fragile one. It was fragile because it was never backed up by the granting of legal rights to peasants. It is true that peasants had escaped many of the traditional burdens of medieval serfdom, but only the minority of peasants who were so-called freeholders of land had a real security against being evicted by the landowner. The aristocracy, as ever, held most of the cards.

11 Agencies of Government

What does the phrase 'agencies of government' mean? In our own times, it might conjure up images of Whitehall departments of state controlled by ministers, armies of civil servants, and cabinets in 10 Downing Street. This is, of course, yet more baggage to be jettisoned. None of these things existed in the 1400s. Loyalty to an abstraction like the 'state' was almost incomprehensible in the fifteenth century. England was a world of personal loyalties which focussed on the king himself. Government meant the personal rule of the king. He would use the network of loyalties between himself, his aristocracy and his royal servants to put his decisions into effect.

a) The King's Council

Nevertheless, no king could make every decision on every matter, and every king needed advice. The king's council fulfilled both these functions. If, for example, the king wanted to launch a military campaign in France, he would sound out the opinions of the council. He might ask his councillors for their views on his aims, the justice of his cause, and his proposed strategy. He might ask them to comment on the likely reaction of Parliament to his plans. But they had no power of veto. If he chose to go to war, then to war the country went. The king's council would then make the arrangements for the summoning, provisioning and despatch of the army. The council could also make decisions on particular issues where the king had already laid down the general policy. It might, for example, interfere in the workings of a town council where it was felt that the king's instructions were not being followed. Similarly, if there were a major breakdown of law and order caused by a quarrel between nobles, the council - operating in effect as a court of law - could (with the king's agreement) step in to sort it out. In 1440, for example, the council had to deal with a violent dispute between the Earl of Devon and Sir William Bonville. It was clear that the Earl was trying to use his own status as a Justice of the Peace to destroy Bonville. There was also an attack made upon an innocent group of merchants who were mistakenly identified as some of Bonville's men. Both Bonville and the Earl had to make assurances of good behaviour to the council.

In times of particular crisis, the king might summon a so-called 'Great Council' at which larger numbers of the nobility than usual would assemble. The aim might be to rally support for the king, or to demonstrate that the king had recovered authority after a rebellion. In 1469, Edward IV summoned just such a council after his release from the custody of the Earl of Warwick (see page 77). And, in an atmosphere of desperate uncertainty caused by the insanity of Henry VI, a Great

Council was called in 1453 to 'set rest and union betwixt the lords of this land'. It might be argued that this disunity had, in large part, been caused by Henry VI when relatively sane. Chapter 3 will examine the fairness or otherwise of this assessment.

Finally, a council might rule without the monarch in very special (and unusual) circumstances. If the king were too young to take the throne, it was possible that a council might rule in his name until he came to his majority (at around 16). This is what happened when Henry V died in 1422 with his son, Henry VI, a nine-month-old baby. Despite the fact that there was no real precedent for rule by council rather than rule by a regent, the council managed it well.

Who became members of the king's council? First, there were the so-called 'natural councillors'. These men were not appointed because they were gifted with profound common-sense or political skills of a high order but simply because they were great nobles. As such, they expected to be consulted by the king. However, it has to be said that a magnate did not always care to attend council regularly. This is not as contradictory as it sounds. If the magnate were reasonably satisfied that his own interests were safe and that the king was reasonably effective, he was likely to think that he could spend time more profitably on his own family and lands. But if those interests did not seem safe, or if the king did not seem to be effective, the magnate needed to be on the council to protect himself. It might be, for example, that the king was being manipulated by a single faction, to which our magnate did not belong. At the very least, the magnate might find himself excluded from the king's patronage if he were not invited to council. In such circumstances he might feel that the rivals who were monopolising that patronage were going to become more powerful while his own power stagnated. Worse, they might slander him, and he would have no way of defending himself to the king. If the worse came to the worst, then the magnate might feel that he had no option but to take violent remedies to force himself on to the council. As a direct result, the stability of whole areas of the country might be threatened. An example of just this situation is discussed in detail in Chapter 3, where the Duke of York saw Henry VI dancing to the tune of York's enemy, the Duke of Suffolk. In 1452, York tried to force his way on to the council, where he intended to assume the leading rôle to which he thought his birth and power entitled him. His chosen method - unsuccessful, in this instance - was to raise an army.

Who were the other members of the council? Given the council's judicial rôle, it is no surprise that judges were frequently councillors. But the largest group - perhaps even larger than the nobles - was often churchmen. Archbishops, bishops, abbots and other senior clerics were especially useful as administrators. To begin with, they were particularly well-educated. Second, since Church law prevented the clergy from marrying, they had no sons or daughters to provide for in the in-fighting at the royal court. In theory, their loyalty to the best interests of the crown ought not be compromised by the loyalty of family. In practice, they often sought to use their position to further family interests. In 1438, Henry Beaufort, Bishop of Winchester, persuaded Henry VI to sell him Chirk Castle in the Welsh Marches (see page 52). The bishop might have used Church money to buy it, but the Church was not going to benefit from it: his own nephews were to find it a suitably tasty addition to their inheritance. Clearly, senior clerics on the council were frequently part of the various noble factions struggling for influence.

It is difficult to give precise figures for the size of the council or for the relative numbers of magnates, other nobles, judges and churchmen. In part, this is because the council attendance lists for this period are seriously incomplete. And in any case, different kings had different policies in selecting councillors, and those policies frequently reflected the king's own power and self-confidence. For example, as Edward IV became more secure on the throne he had taken from Henry VI, he employed fewer magnates and senior clergymen of noble origin: instead, he introduced men he had promoted from the ranks of the gentry and on whose loyalty he had reason to rely (see page 121).

From what has been said so far, it should be clear that it was absolutely vital for a king to control his council. A council that was ripped apart by factional fighting, or a council that was dominated by one faction, could destabilise the whole country. Its quarrels and decisions were bound to have a knock-on effect in the various areas of the country controlled by the members of the factions. But the king's task of control was not an easy one. To begin with, he had to select councillors to achieve a balance between the factions. But he also had to recognise where one noble's strength in land gave him the right to a greater standing in the council than others. This meant that the king had to be seen to listen with particular care to the advice offered by this noble. But at no point could he afford to lose his freedom of action. And, like Edward IV, he needed to be able to include those whose position on the council was entirely dependent on the goodwill of the king. Finally, the king had to have the force of character to impose himself on a council when he attended its meetings. He also had to have sufficient self-confidence to allow it to meet without his constant and direct supervision.

The king did have important advantages as he sought to control his council. As we have seen, he chose and appointed the councillors. If necessary, he dismissed them. In any case, it was up to him to decide how large the council was to be. He could manipulate the numbers to counteract an attempt by any faction to gain predominance. And, in the end, the council could do little without the explicit authority of the king. For example, Edward IV faced major insurrection in 1464. His council (in London) responded by trying to raise money by selling licences granting merchants permission to trade in wool. But absolutely nothing could be done without the king's written authority, and that had to be obtained despite the dangerous delay (the king being in Yorkshire at the time). In fact, no decisions requiring written orders or instructions could be made without the king's signature (the so-called 'sign manual') and signet (the king's seal).

b) The Royal Household

The king, as we have seen, was the most important focus of power in fifteenth-century England. The council was another important focus. A third was the court: and the heart of the king's court was the royal household. What did the household actually do? At its most basic level, it fed, clothed, entertained and exhibited the king in appropriately magnificent style. The king's chamber was at the centre of the household, and was a suite of rooms providing his living quarters. His secretary and the clerks of the signet were also based in the chamber, ready at hand to draw up whatever written instructions the king required. The Lord Chamberlain supervised the work of the chamber, but his most significant task in political terms was to control access to the king. This was important, since the king's world, strangely enough, was not a large one. To an extent, he saw it through the eyes and heard it through the ears of those closest to him. The point is that access to the king meant influence, and influence might mean manipulation, and manipulation might mean a distortion of the king's power. Potentially, this could be dangerous. There was the danger - as Fortescue stressed - that the king might make policy decisions based less on discussion in council and more on whispers in the household. It was easy to fall into this trap, since the key members of the household accompanied kings on their frequent travels. The council generally remained at its Westminster base.

One of the most useful sources for historians of fifteenth-century England is the Paston letters. Seeking to defend their interests against local rivals, the Pastons knew of no better way than to mobilise whatever contacts they had in or around the household. In this way, the king might be persuaded to favour them in their struggles. In 1479, for example, John Paston III tried to enlist the aid of 'Sir George Browne, Sir James Radcliff, and other of mine acquaintance which wait most upon the king and lie nightly in his chamber'. This represents just one attempt to influence the king, who had to contend with a barrage of requests, petitions, pleadings for patronage as distilled through his courtiers. The following letter from John Paston II to his father is an instructive example. The issue involves the Pastons' property at Dedham, which had been seized by the Duke of Suffolk.

1 I laboured daily my Lord of Essex, Treasurer of England, to have moved the King ... he answered me that he had felt and moved the

King therein, rehearsing the King's answer therein ... he [the King]
said he would be your good lord therein as he would be to the
5 poorest man in England. He would hold with you in your right;
and as for favour, he will not understand that he shall show favour
more to one man than to another, not to one in England ... My
Lord of Essex saith he will do as much for you as for any esquire in
England, and Baronners his man telleth [me], saying, 'Your father
10 is much beholding to my lord, for he loveth him well.' Baronners
moved me once and said that ye must needs do somewhat for my
lord and his ...

No king, then, could afford to be unaware of the possible implications of
factional intrigue in the corridors and rooms of the household. But he
also had to be aware of the need to make the household an exhibition of
the power and majesty of the monarch. The king was expected to behave
like a king and to look like a king. This meant generosity and
magnificent hospitality. It also meant that the physical presence of the
king should be impressive. His manner, his dignity and his appearance
should communicate the supposed power and wealth of his country,
together with suitable overtones of military skill and personal strength.
Foreign ambassadors had to be impressed, and so did the common
people. Solemn processions and other ceremonials were weapons used
to demonstrate the prestige of the king, but they could - and did -
backfire. In 1471, a distinctly feeble Henry VI went on procession from
St Paul's Cathedral in a blue robe that had seen better days. Londoners
who saw him scarcely bothered to conceal their sneers.

c) Parliament

What was a fifteenth-century Parliament, and what power did it have?
Parliament was made up of Lords and Commons (not 'House of Lords'
or 'House of Commons' - these terms were not current in the fifteenth
century). The Lords consisted of the Lords temporal and Lords
spiritual: in other words, peers (the five upper ranks of the nobility -
barons, viscounts, earls, marquesses and dukes) and senior churchmen
(archbishops, bishops, and the more important abbots and priors). By
no means all those eligible to attend and summoned by writ bothered to
do so. The Lords, together with a professional administrative council
appointed by the king, were in sole possession of the parliament house.
The Commons occupied a separate chamber. The Commons consisted
of knights (gentry, in other words) and burgesses. Two knights were
elected for each of the shires (counties), the burgesses by the boroughs
(towns), although some gentry also sought election for the boroughs.
Elections for knights and burgesses were in no sense democratic. In fact,
the majority of seats were not even contested. In the boroughs, the
variety of franchises (the qualification needed to be able to vote) was

remarkable, but it was frequently the case that only the aldermen and councillors possessed it. The deliberations of the Commons were controlled by a Speaker, who, although he was elected by the Commons, was almost invariably a royal servant. The equivalent function in the Lords was carried out by the Lord Chancellor.

In twentieth-century terms, a fifteenth-century Parliament could not be seen as very representative. A body of men voicing the concerns of major landowners and the propertied classes of the towns, yes: but as an institution reflecting the needs of all the people, rich or poor, young and old, men and women - absolutely not. But in fifteenth-century terms, Parliament was truly representative, in that it represented the views of people that mattered. The poor had no stake in the country since they owned little or no property in it. It would, therefore, be quite wrong to canvass their views. This does not mean that the condition of the poor would be ignored, if only because a discontented populace threatened property. But it does mean that they had no direct access to political power.

How much power did Parliament have? The fifteenth-century Parliament was a royal institution. Its purpose was to assist with the implementation - and not the making - of royal policy. Parliament had no existence independent of the king's will. He summoned it whenever he wished, prorogued it (terminated a session) whenever it served his needs, and dissolved it whenever it had fulfilled the purpose for which it had been called. That purpose was normally to provide the king with money.

However, Parliament was not some sort of ceremonial audience-chamber where the king practised his public-speaking and its members the difficult art of yawning with one's mouth shut while opening one's purse at the king's request. Strictly speaking, the king could not impose taxes on the laity (those not in the employ of the Church) without the agreement of the Commons. The king had no right to taxes (or to customs duties) just because he was king. In fact, it was generally thought that the king should, under normal circumstances, 'live of his own'. In other words, he should rely on his income from his massive crown lands and feudal dues to run the country. Only in an emergency should the Commons be asked to agree to taxation. To take an example, in 1463, Edward IV called a Parliament with a request for money to lead an army against the Scots. The Commons reminded the king that the money was to be used for that purpose and no other, and was less than pleased when Edward failed to keep his word. Later requests for money for wars with France (see page 136) were greeted with suspicion, and grants were hedged about with reminders of the king's duty to maintain law and order. In particular, the Parliament of 1472 arranged for the tax to be collected and held in safe-keeping until the king was ready to sail for France. If he had not done so by a certain date, then the money was to be returned to the taxpayers. This, however, falls short of an absolute right to refuse taxation. The Commons might try to reduce the amount demanded, or hedge it about with restrictions (as we have seen). But a point-blank refusal was unlikely in the extreme.

The king could not make, amend or repeal laws without parliamentary consent. As with taxation, it was not easy to envisage Parliament refusing a king's legislation. However, in a crisis, it was possible that the Commons might itself seek to push through legislation that members knew did not meet with the king's wishes, even though it was not possible to criticise the king directly or seek to diminish his power. For example, in 1450, the Commons attempted to impeach (accuse of treason) the Duke of Suffolk and then pass a bill declaring his guilt (see page 44). Henry VI was obliged to defend his favourite, but could do no more to protect him than send him into exile. This aggressive behaviour on the part of the Commons was very unusual, and must have reflected a deep concern about the state of the country.

To summarise: Parliament was, under normal circumstances, most definitely not a threat to the power of a king. Its own powers were very limited. These could be manipulated by the king through his use of the Speaker, through his influence over the Lords, and through the simple fact that Parliament sat as and when he required it. After all, Parliament was very useful to the king: it was an extremely convenient mechanism for getting money out of his subjects. A sensible king could also use it to gauge the country's reaction to his policies. This is not to say that the Commons might not prove troublesome if it doubted a king's good faith in requesting money: but the money still, in general, came through. However, there is one important proviso here. The Commons could take on a rôle that amounted to opposition to a king if the country slumped into a major crisis as a result of the policies he was following. If the king needed money very badly, he would find it difficult to react to Parliament's opposition by simply dissolving it. In this kind of situation it might be possible for a magnate to use Parliament as a weapon of factional intrigue. The Commons might be persuaded to present the king with a petition of grievances in which the magnates' enemies would be heavily censured. Once again, we see the importance of the king securing the right relationship with all his nobility.

12 Law and Disorder

The fifteenth-century aristocracy was obsessed with the law. As Professor Bellamy suggested in his *Bastard Feudalism and the Law,* 'Very few indeed of the men and women of gentry status and above ... did not appear as either plaintiff or defendant in the courts ... at some time in their lives'. And yet, these very people were as frequently attempting to interfere with the course of justice. It was the aristocracy's behaviour which most threatened the rule of law itself. What explanation can be offered? The simple answer is - land. The search for it, the need to safeguard it, the desire to add to it, and the attempt to hand it over to heirs without paying reliefs or allowing rivals to challenge for it: land dominated the thinking of the aristocracy. The complexity of the laws surrounding inheritance and land law itself fuelled both the legal battles and the force frequently used to further one's claims. It was a violent time, and one good and favoured way to press a claim was to attack an opponent's manor house. He and his retainers would be thrown out, and the aggressor would occupy it himself before settling down for the legal battle. To be fair, it was unusual for deaths to result or for property to be damaged intentionally. Nevertheless, there are exceptions - as the two cases below suggest.

The following is a petition presented to Parliament in 1450 by John Paston I. Paston's manor at Gresham in Norfolk had been seized by Lord Moleyns. While he was attempting to recover his manor, Paston took a house in Gresham. At this point

1 the said lord [Moleyns] sent to the said mansion a riotous people, to the number of 1,000 persons ... arrayed in manner of war ... and so came into the said mansion ... and mined down the wall of the chamber wherein the wife of your said beseecher was, and bore her
5 out at the gates ... and broke up all chambers and coffers within the said mansion and ... in manner of robbery bore away all the stuff, array, and money that your said beseecher and his servants had there ...

This is a petition presented to Parliament in 1455 by John Radford, cousin of the Nicholas Radford of the text.

1 To the king our sovereign lord ... the Thursday the 23rd day of October ... there [to Nicholas Radford's property in Devon] came Thomas Courtenay ... son to Thomas Earl of Devonshire ... with other riotous persons ... As soon as these misdoers had beset the
5 place they made a great shout there and set the gates of the said place afire. And the said Nicholas awoke and opened his window of his chamber ... And then the said Sir Thomas Courtenay ... called to him, saying in this wise, 'Come down Radford and speak with me.' And then the said Nicholas Radford ... answered ... 'Sir, if you
10 will promise me on your faith and truth, and as you are a true knight and a gentleman, that I shall have no bodily harm nor hurt of my goods, I will come down to you.'

[Courtenay duly promises: but, once the doors are open, Radford is robbed.]

1 And the said Nicholas Radford seeing so many people within his said house, was sore afraid, and said to Sir Thomas Courtenay

knight, 'Sir, what are all these people doing here?' and he answered
again and said 'Radford, you shall have no harm'....And then
5 afterwards the said Thomas Courtenay. ... said to him 'Have done
Radford, for thou must go with me to my Lord my father' .... .and
.... the said Sir Thomas Courtenay knight talked privately with the
said Nicholas Philip, Thomas Philip, and John Amore, and
forthwith spurred his horse, and rode his way and said 'Fare well,
10 Radford'. And the said Nicholas Philip ... smote the said Nicholas
Radford a hideous deadly stroke across the face, and felled him to
the ground, and then the said Nicholas Philip gave him another
stroke behind his head so that his brains fell out....And
forthwith...the said Sir Thomas Courtenay with all the said
15 misdoers rode to Tiverton...where the said Earl...feloniously
received, comforted, and harboured (them)'

According to the cousin's account, what happened next was that
Thomas Courtenay's younger brother arrived to conduct an inquest on
the murder. He pinned it on a group of fictitious people and then
crushed the body with stones to hamper any proper inquest. All the
Courtenays later sought and were granted a pardon from the king.

The relationship between the aristocracy and the law was further
complicated by the fact that the king inevitably relied upon the
aristocracy for the actual administration of justice in the localities. The
sheriff - invariably a member of the gentry - was the main agent
responsible for the operation of the local courts. His rôle included the
arrest of offenders and their despatch to the appropriate courts. One of
his most important tasks was to approve the choice of a jury at the
twice-yearly 'tourns' or sheriff's law days. Since the verdict of a jury
might, on occasion, lead to the loss of the entire inheritance of a suitor,
many landowners saw it as more than necessary to attempt to influence
the sheriff to ensure a suitably sympathetic jury. The practice of bribing
a jury was known as embracery. Alternatively, jurors could simply be
overawed by, say, the fortuitous presence of armed men loitering about
the court wearing the livery (badge or uniform) of a lord whose retainer
just happened to be a plaintiff or defendant in the case. As explained on
page 23, the practice of influencing the provision of justice through
pressure, intimidation, force or the threat of force was known as
maintenance.

The next stage up the legal hierarchy was occupied by the justices of
the peace. At their quarter sessions, justices of the peace heard only
criminal cases (not cases brought by individuals) connected with land
and contracts of various types. They also dealt with such felonies as
robbery and murder. But, once again, JPs were usually members of the
gentry. Kings did sometimes appoint magnates to improve the prestige
of the JPs and to reduce the chance of their being pressured by local
interests. But it was, in fact, rare for magnates to serve in person. There

are, significantly, cases where JPs were clearly intimidated by a powerful noble. One notorious case involved none other than George, Duke of Clarence, the younger brother of Edward IV. In 1477, Clarence forced the Warwick JPs to indict three entirely innocent people for the alleged murder of his wife. The jury were then 'persuaded' to find them guilty, which they duly did out of fear of the consequences. The three unfortunates were immediately executed (see page 141).

Criminal justice was particularly weak. It was extremely difficult to get offenders to court, even if the sheriff exerted himself. And, even then, securing a conviction was even more difficult. As described by Charles Ross, the Shropshire Peace Roll for 1400-14 contains some revealing statistics. The JPs of that shire indicted 251 people for felony (conviction for which generally carried the death penalty). Of these, 156 were summoned to the prestigious court of King's Bench, but only 14 subsequently stood trial. How many were convicted? Not one.

Even if conviction were likely, it was possible to avoid it by obtaining a writ (a legal command) of *supersedeas*. This writ was well worth having. We might consider the case of a gentleman clearly guilty of a felony. He has been unable to influence the jury or the Justice of the Peace, and it looks as though he is going to be one of the very few to suffer the full penalty under the law. But he then produces a writ of *supersedeas* - and the trial is simply halted permanently. In this case, our hypothetical gentleman would probably have obtained it (i.e. bought it) from the king. It was also possible to obtain one from JPs. In the unlikely event of a conviction, a well-connected person could always approach the king for a pardon. Some kings - Henry VI being a particularly notorious example - were all too ready to grant royal pardons (sometimes for money). In so doing, they were effectively sabotaging the system for which they were ultimately responsible.

This is not to say that the many breakdowns in law and order can, therefore, be blamed directly on a king. It is worth reminding ourselves that, in a society dominated by a military ruling class, it was inevitable that a considerable level of violence was an accepted fact of life. Law and violence were favourite means of settling quarrels, but it is significant that few people seem to have seen them as mutually exclusive. A member of the aristocracy who wanted his own way might use the law, or force, or both. Lacking a police force and/or a standing army, the king was forced to rely on those who were unlikely to be impartial. It is an exaggeration to say that the law was in the control of the criminals, but, like all exaggerations, there is an element of truth in it. In any case, the king's interest in law and order was limited. So long as there were no major and widespread breakdowns of public order or acts of defiance of royal authority; so long as the king's revenue was not affected; so long as traitors were not harboured - then the king would be reasonably satisfied with his performance. After all, it would not do to forfeit the goodwill and support of his magnates by probing too deeply into a spot of corruption or maintenance or embracery on their part. There were plenty of laws in fifteenth-century England. It was putting them into effect that was so difficult.

Finally, the link between political stability and law and order needs to be made explicit. If a weak king failed to control his nobles, then the legal system inevitably suffered. The Courtenay and Radford case shows what might happen if powerful nobles felt that they had little to fear from the law. And, of course, the reason why they did not fear the law was because they did not fear the king. As we have seen, nobles were often inclined to behave as if the legal system existed to further their own interests. Only an effective king could stop their blatant exploitation of the law.

13 Conclusion on the Rôle of the King

Our discussion of English society in the fifteenth century has demonstrated that the calibre of a king was probably the most important single element in ensuring the relative stability and security of the country. It therefore makes sense to spell out the characteristics of the ideal king, most of which underpin the previous sections of this chapter. These will prove useful as criteria to assess the kings and would-be kings of the period of the Wars of the Roses.

In the first place, an effective king should have a certain charisma. There were times when all and sundry needed to be reminded of his authority. A commanding presence was essential. When he showed himself to his people, he had to be impressive. Given the king's rôle as defender of the country, he needed to be an able military tactician. More importantly, he needed to be able to fight in person. Cowardice or lack of interest in the battlefield were serious shortcomings. He was expected to protect the Church, although an excess of religious zeal was unlikely to be thought of as a kingly trait by the hard-headed nobility. The king needed the benefit of good health to provide effective leadership. There were occasions - perhaps a major breakdown in law and order - that required an energetic and immediate input from the king.

Perhaps the most challenging aspect of the rôle of the king was his relationship with the aristocracy, and particularly with the magnates. In dealing with the aristocracy, the king faced a task of staggering complexity. Much of the complexity arose from the contradictions within the power-structure of the kingdom. First, he was set above all his subjects by his God-given status. But, in practice, he relied upon the military support of his aristocracy to maintain his power. Second, he had to be able to impose his own authority on the magnates. Yet, he also had to be prepared to listen and to respect their advice. Third, although he had to make sure that he did not allow any one faction to dominate himself, his kingdom or his council, he had to recognise - and show that he recognised - that some nobles were more powerful than others. Such men had to feel that their advice was particularly welcome to the king. If the king failed to get his relationship with the aristocracy right, then the system of justice (such as it was) was fatally compromised. Get it wrong, and major disorder could follow. It could take the form of assaults on a dominant faction with which the king was identified. If the worse came to the worst, the rebellion might be against the king himself.

What personal qualities, then, did a king need to control his aristocracy? Self-confidence was essential. A timid or indecisive monarch would be submerged in the potent rivalries of court and council. He clearly needed to be an excellent judge of character. He would have to be able to understand the personal strengths and weaknesses of his nobles, because these would need to be channelled and exploited to control factional rivalries. To do this, ruthlessness was a distinct advantage. The aristocracy needed to respect the king. This respect would partly come from a feeling that the king identified with their values and obsessions (i.e. land and inheritance). But it would come mainly from fear. A noble had to feel that the king would punish disloyalty by exploiting the ultimate weapon from his feudal armoury: the right to deprive a traitor of his lands and life.

A lazy king was not a good king. Effective personal monarchy meant that a king had the energy to intervene where necessary in the quarrels and antagonisms at court. It also meant personal supervision. He had to make sure that the various crown revenues - income from the crown lands, feudal dues and so on - were being efficiently collected. If not, then the king had less patronage to offer a loyal nobility: and a king was expected to be generous. The ability to offer this generous patronage, together with the common-sense to use it shrewdly, were vital tools in the king's political manoeuvres with the nobility.

Did such a king ever exist? He is clearly being expected to perform a remarkable balancing act of near-superhuman proportions. In the fifteenth century, perhaps Henry V came the closest to this ideal king. It is one of the bitterest ironies that his son, Henry VI, lacked almost every one of his father's attributes.

Making notes on '*England in the Mid-Fifteenth Century*'

As section 1 suggests, the aim of this chapter is to provide you with the necessary understanding of how English society worked. This is to help you deal with questions on the causes of the Wars, the impact of the Wars and Yorkist government. You may find it helpful to revisit this chapter when you need a reminder of the concepts encountered in later chapters. The good news is that you should aim to keep notes as brief as possible. Some sections will not require notes at all.

1.   What was the kingdom of England?

1.1   What was the relationship between England, Scotland, France and Ireland?

1.2   How did the king deal with Wales and the north?

2.   England, France and the Hundred Years War

2.1   What were English motives in the Hundred Years War?

3.   The Hundred Years War and National Identity

3.1   What evidence is there that a sense of national identity was developing in the fifteenth century?

4.   The structure of English society - an introduction
      Notes not required.

5.   The rôle of the king

5.1   What was the purpose of kingship? What were the powers of the king? Make sure you define the following:
      a) prerogatives
      b) patronage

6.   The Nobility: a definition

6.1   What is the difference between peer, magnate and gentleman?

7.   The nobility and the king

7.1   Feudalism. Explain the workings of feudalism, making sure you use the following terms:
      a) feudal contract
      b) the feudal rights (or 'incidents') of relief and wardship
      c) retaining
      d) attainder

7.2   Bastard feudalism. Define. Makes sure you refer to maintenance and livery.

8.   The Church. Notes not needed.

9.   The cities, towns and trade

9.1   What was the economic and political importance of towns and the merchant class?

10.   The Labourers

10.1 How much power did the labourers possess?

11.   Agencies of government

11.1 Describe the function of:
      a) the king's council
      b) the Great Council
      c) the royal household
      d) Parliament.

12.   Law and disorder

12.1 In what way did the behaviour of the aristocracy threaten the rule of law?

12.2 In what way was criminal justice weak, and why?

12.3 Why and in what way was the king's interest in justice limited?

13.   Conclusion on the rôle of the king

13.1 What were the personal qualities of an effective king?

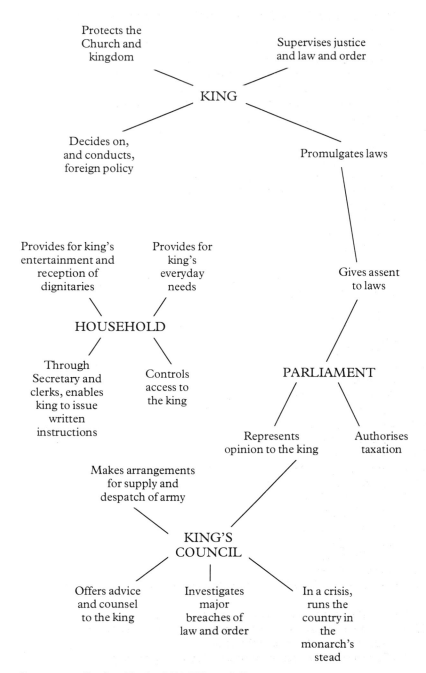

Protects the
Church and
kingdom

Supervises justice
and law and order

KING

Decides on,
and conducts,
foreign policy

Promulgates laws

Provides for king's
entertainment and
reception of
dignitaries

Provides for
king's
everyday
needs

Gives assent
to laws

HOUSEHOLD

Through
Secretary and
clerks, enables
king to issue
written
instructions

Controls
access to
the king

PARLIAMENT

Represents
opinion to the king

Authorises
taxation

Makes arrangements
for supply and
despatch of army

KING'S
COUNCIL

Offers advice
and counsel
to the king

Investigates
major
breaches of
law and order

In a crisis,
runs the
country in
the
monarch's
stead

Summary - England in the Mid-Fifteenth Century

Source-based questions on 'England in the Mid-Fifteenth Century'

1 John Radford's petition to Parliament, 1465
Study the extract on pages 35-6. Answer the following questions.
a) Write an argument in favour of the reliability of the petition. (3 marks)
b) Write an argument against the reliability of the petition. (3 marks)
c) How might an historian use the petition in assessing and describing the state of law and order in fifteenth-century England? (4 marks)

CHAPTER 3

The Downfall of Henry VI

1 Introduction

In the introduction to Chapter 1, it was suggested that history - in the sense of the past - does not exist. We have no way of persuading the past to return, and we cannot (thank goodness) relive it. So, history itself is our attempt to make sense of the past by imposing some sort of order on it that appears to us meaningful. In the case of this chapter, we shall be looking at that part of the Wars of the Roses from the attempts of the Duke of York to take what he saw as his rightful place at the court of Henry VI to the eventual coronation of York's son who, as Edward IV, usurped the throne from Henry VI. Chapter 4 will look at the stabilising of Edward's régime following the final defeat and death of Henry VI. It will also examine the usurpation of the throne by Edward IV's brother, Richard of Gloucester, who took the title of Richard III.

It should be stressed that there is nothing inevitable or automatic about dividing up the Wars of the Roses in this way. The division reflects a particular interpretation: namely, that the causes of the sets of conflicts were by no means identical. And so, it is important for students writing essays on the Wars of the Roses to avoid the assumption that examiners will accept this division without being given a justification of it.

2 A Narrative of Events

The astute student reader might have noted the comments about examiners and then be surprised to see a section devoted to mere narrative. After all, do not examiners particularly dislike narrative devoid of argument? This is true enough: but this section is intended simply to give shape to a complex set of events, many of which seem, at first sight, to involve a bewildering variety of people with identical names and near-identical titles. Many a student of this period has reason to bemoan the apparent popularity of the names Edward, Richard and Henry among the royal family and upper nobility. The family tree on page 2 will need frequent revisiting.

In 1422, Henry of Windsor, a nine-month-old baby, became King of England as Henry VI. His warrior father, Henry V, had succumbed to dysentery - as deadly to the medieval soldier as a crossbow bolt. In 1431, Henry VI was crowned King of France as well. His English lands and his crown were well served by the royal council that governed in his name, and, when he took full control of his kingdom by 1437, the monarch's powers were undiminished and his inheritance more or less intact. By 1450, virtually everything possible had gone wrong. The king had shown little interest in war. Disastrous failures in the field led to the loss of

Normandy to the French in 1450 and of Gascony the next year: only Calais remained of the English king's possessions in his second kingdom. At home, the king apparently deluged the court factions he favoured with crown offices and lands. He allowed the Earl of Suffolk (made a duke in 1448) to dominate the Royal Household and stood by him when he was accused by the Commons of treason over the disasters in France. In fact, Henry's attempt to save Suffolk misfired when the ship carrying him to the safety of exile was intercepted. Suffolk was then beheaded by the sailors of the ship *Nicholas of the Tower* in April 1450. The Commons also attempted to get the king to claw back all the grants - of crown lands and the like - which he had unwisely scattered among his favourites and so weakened the crown itself. An Act of Resumption - humiliating to the king - was duly passed in the May of 1450, and was followed later in the same month by the so-called Cade rebellion. This is best seen as a kind of armed petition to the king, supporting the Commons' efforts to destroy the dominant faction around Henry. The rebels' demands are significant: they wanted punishment for the alleged misdeeds of various royal servants in Kent (where many of the rebels came from); they wanted fairer justice; they wanted the destruction of the remains of the Suffolk faction; and they wanted Henry to rely upon the advice of other great lords whose voices were rarely heard at the king's council. In particular, they singled out Richard, Duke of York, who was of royal blood and seen by some as the childless Henry's heir. Cade's rebellion eventually collapsed: but not before the king had demonstrated a weakness bordering on cowardice in fleeing from his capital.

In September 1450, York returned unbidden from his virtual exile as Lieutenant of Ireland. He had no links with the Cade rebellion, but was no doubt anxious to make this abundantly clear. He also hoped to take on what he saw as his rightful place in the king's council as his chief minister. But Henry was now relying upon Edmund Beaufort, Duke of Somerset, despite the latter's conspicuous failures as the defeated and last Lieutenant of Normandy. York brooded heavily in his power-base in the Welsh Marches, and decided to try to impose himself on the king by a display of force. In 1452, his army was met by a stronger royal force at Dartford. York had no choice but to submit himself to Henry. On his knees, he presented the unimpressed and unresponsive king with a long list of complaints about Somerset, but was obliged to swear an oath of allegiance to Henry in St Paul's Cathedral.

For a short time things seemed to be improving for the king. There were military successes in Gascony in 1453, and Henry was displaying signs of what appeared to be genuine energy and commitment. However, the next signs he displayed were of undeniable insanity, possibly triggered by the news that his commander in Gascony, the Earl of Shrewsbury, had been defeated and killed in battle at Castillon: Gascony was lost once and for all. Henry was in some sort of stupor, incapable of communicating and scarcely able to use his limbs. From August 1453 to January 1455, he could not rule his kingdom. The kingdom had to be ruled - but how? There was, after all, the problem of York to consider. As a great noble in his own right, he ought to be summoned to a Great Council to help deal with the crisis. The birth of a son to Henry and his queen, Margaret of Anjou, both complicated the situation and made it easier. It was easier because York was now no longer heir presumptive to the throne, and could not therefore claim to be regent: a position he would no doubt relish as the chance to avenge himself on his many enemies at court. It was complicated by the fact that the energetic and strong-minded Margaret of Anjou clearly saw York as the major threat to her infant son, Edward, and would destroy him if possible. The Council could not accept Margaret's attempts to become regent herself, and conferred the office of Protector and Defender of England on York in March 1454. York had made sure that his chief rival Somerset had been committed to the Tower of London in November 1453, and now tried to have him put on trial for alleged treasonable failures in France. However, Henry's recovery meant that York's Protectorship was at an end. Somerset was released, declared innocent of any charges, and restored to favour. In other words, Henry VI had signalled his intention of returning to his old favourites, his old factions and his old ways. York and his allies withdrew from court, expecting trouble. Their only real chance was to impose their will on the king by force. Protesting their loyalty but demanding the right to remove 'traitors' from the king's presence, York and his supporters the Nevilles faced the outnumbered forces of the king at St Albans in May 1455. In the resulting skirmish, they made sure that Somerset did not leave the city alive. The Earl of Northumberland was also killed, and these deaths meant that the opposing factions were no longer just bitter political rivals; they were opponents in a blood-feud. Henry was now in York's hands, and suffered (unsurprisingly) a relapse. York was once again Protector until the king's relative recovery in February 1456 when, briefly and uncharacteristically, Henry had the good sense to keep York in a prominent rôle. But the queen had other ideas. In all probability, she persuaded Henry that York was aiming for the throne. In 1459, a Great Council in the Lancastrian midland stronghold of Coventry indicted York and Richard Neville, Earl of Warwick, for treason. The Yorkist response was the usual one - to protest loyalty and to raise an army. But this time, they were faced with superior forces at Ludford in Shropshire: York fled to Ireland and Warwick to Calais.

In November 1459, the Lancastrians called a parliament at Coventry. This so-called 'Parliament of the Devils' found the Yorkists guilty of treason, sentenced them to death in their absence and - in an unusually vicious move - 'corrupted the blood' in an act of attainder which prevented their lands from being inherited by their heirs. The Yorkists had no alternative but to fight, and an army under Warwick and

Edward, Earl of March (York's eldest son) defeated the king's forces at Northampton in July 1460: Henry VI himself was captured. As York returned from Ireland, he marched for the first time under a royal banner and, arriving at the assembling of Parliament in Westminster Hall, he made a dramatic gesture. By placing his hand on the throne, he signalled his intention to claim the kingship by right. If he expected support, he was to be disappointed. There followed an embarrassing period where York demanded an immediate decision on his claim from the Lords in Parliament. The Lords hastily referred the matter to Henry himself, and then to the king's justices, who referred it back - until, in the end, the Lords came up with a frankly unworkable compromise known inappropriately as the Act of Accord. Henry VI was to retain the throne, but his son, Edward, was to be disinherited and York was to be his heir.

For one thing, this compromise failed to take account of the energy of Queen Margaret. Raising forces in the north, in Wales and the west country, she was a formidable threat. York set out to challenge the queen, but was killed in a skirmish outside his own castle of Sandal in Yorkshire. The queen's army turned its attention to Warwick, who was defeated at the second battle of St Albans. Henry VI was rescued. But York's son Edward (now Duke of York, of course) was still at large. He was able to enter London in February 1461 and had sufficient support to claim the title of king, on the grounds that Henry VI had broken his agreement with Richard of York.

It was all very well for Edward (now Edward IV) to go through a suitably shortened and hasty coronation: what he needed to do was decisively to defeat the Lancastrians on the field of battle. This is exactly what he did at Towton (near Tadcaster) on 29 March 1461. Margaret, Henry and their son Edward fled to Scotland. Edward IV now had the leisure to return to London for a proper coronation. Prince Edward was safely ensconced in France, but Henry VI led a curious wandering life around and about the borders with Scotland until he was captured by Yorkists in July 1465. He was lodged in the Tower of London - safe enough, since Edward IV was sufficiently astute to realise that the former king's death at his hands would simply provide the Lancastrians with useful propaganda. And - to be uncharitable - the Lancastrian cause could only gain from the replacement of an ineffectual monarch with a son who showed much more promise.

3 Causes of the Downfall of Henry VI

Even in the narrative of the previous section, opinions on the causes of events kept obtruding themselves. This is inevitable, since narrative without causation is like a story minus a plot. Without an analysis of causes, political history would be no more than a list of events without shape or meaning. Providing nothing more than a list of causes would also be bad history. What we need to do is to impose some sort of structure on our explanation of causes. One widely-accepted method is to divide up the causes into those that are long-term and those that are short-term. This is useful, because it helps us to identify which causes were reflections of problems stemming from the structure of medieval society (usually the long-term causes) and which reflected specific events or, perhaps, personalities (usually the short-term causes). This would still be a list, albeit a more sophisticated one. So, some judgment of relative importance is needed (sometimes known as a 'hierarchy of factors'). Hopefully, the following discussion will provide an example of this approach at work.

a) Long-term Causes

i) Had there been a long-term shift in power away from the king and towards the nobility?

Indeed there had. The early fourteenth century was characterised by struggles for power between king and nobility. Edward I (r. 1272-1307) generally increased royal power, but his son, Edward II (r. 1307-27), paid the price in strife that led to his murder. Under Edward III (r. 1327-77), the relationship stabilised, but at some cost to the potential authority of subsequent kings. First, Edward III successfully channelled the energies of his nobility into the military campaigns in France which marked the start of the Hundred Years War. But, in return for their support, he made concessions which effectively increased the power of the nobility. Nobles played a greater role in the enforcement of justice through membership of commissions of the peace. And the magnates were encouraged to provide themselves with a permanent circle of armed retainers as a mark of their prestige. In addition, he created a new, upper nobility: a magnate class which was given the opportunity to marry into the royal family, and which was offered new titles (such as duke) to enhance its status.

There were potential dangers to royal authority in creating a class of nobles of the blood royal. Such nobles expected to have a near-monopoly of influence over the king. Important councillors and ministers who were not of royal stock would find their influence resented. The Cade rebels of 1450 asked that Henry should 'take about his noble person his true blood of his royal realm, that is to say, the high and mighty prince the Duke of York' and went on to list other cousins of the king. In 1469, Edward IV's brother, George, Duke of Clarence and Richard Neville, Earl of Warwick made barbed comments about the kings who had been weak and unsuccessful. Their failure was caused, apparently, by the fact that they had 'estranged the great lords of their blood from their secret counsel, and not advised by them; and taking about them other not of their blood, and inclining only to their counsel, rule and advice'.

This legacy from Edward III required careful handling by any king. He might well have to perform a tricky balancing act between the inevitable expectations of his noble kinsmen and the need to preserve a necessary freedom of action, which itself would include the choosing of his own councillors and intimates. But, providing this could be done, there was no necessary conflict of interests between the increasingly powerful nobility and the king. As we have already seen, no king could rule alone. A strong and effective nobility, bound to the king with ties of blood, mutual respect and interest, need not lessen royal power. It could even increase that power. But the crucial factor here is the king himself. If the king lacked the intelligence, dynamism and charisma necessary to reconcile his own interest with those of the nobility, then trouble would not be far away. If he allowed one faction to dominate others - particularly if those excluded from his favour and counsels included men of the blood royal - there was real danger of conflict. It will be argued in section b. that Henry VI conspicuously lacked those qualities. In his case, the awkward but by no means unmanageable legacy of increased noble power was transformed into a major cause of instability as magnates sought to attain or retain what they saw as their rightful position of influence over the king. Even then, attempts by some magnates to impose themselves on the king need not have lead to his downfall. Henry VI's failure to meet the real challenges posed by the power of the nobility does not in itself explain the attempt by Richard of York to depose him. Clearly there are other factors involved; and these will be examined in later sections of the chapter.

ii) How important was bastard feudalism as a cause of the Wars of the Roses?

Bastard feudalism was defined on page 23. There are a number of possible interpretations of the relationship between bastard feudalism and the Wars of the Roses that need examination.

First, any argument that the wars came about as a direct result of bastard feudalism can be dismissed. There is no reason why the practice of substituting a money fee for land to acquire a retainer should threaten kingship itself or the throne of Henry VI in particular. This may seem a surprising view, if one were to accept that bastard feudalism at least gave a great noble the chance to increase the number of his armed supporters. In times of war - say, the French campaigns - bastard feudalism certainly gave a noble the opportunity to increase his armed retinue quickly and conveniently. But, setting aside major foreign adventures, the evidence suggests that nobles as frequently retained administrators by money fee as they did men at arms. And it would be a gross distortion to assume that their men at arms were constantly wandering the countryside looking for violent ways to further their lords' interests. Their presence in a noble's household was sufficient testimony to his prestige, and they did not need to be armed to the teeth and dripping with someone else's blood to make the point. In any case, a magnate's influence was not restricted to indentured retainers. Members of the nobility were constantly seeking to manipulate contacts with the great lords through a more informal network of loyalty than that provided by bastard feudalism. A member of the gentry could hope for a magnate to be his 'good lord' and a magnate could expect, in return, the services of a 'well-willer' on the basis of mutual support in the inevitable local and legal rivalries of fifteenth century society.

Secondly, from what has already been said, it should be clear that the argument that bastard feudalism was inherently de-stabilising should be rejected. The behaviour of nobles could and did threaten the king's peace and the effectiveness of the judicial system, but bastard feudalism neither encouraged nor discouraged such threats. As A.J. Pollard has argued, it was not so much the use of ordinary retainers that led to major breakdowns in law and order, but more the decision of some nobles to recruit thugs to assist in a particular quarrel. John Talbot, Earl of Shrewsbury, is Pollard's example. It seems that this magnate decided to use force against Lord Grey of Codnor, and handed out his badge (a white dog) to some suitably violent locals for the duration of the conflict. This is less bastard feudalism than gang warfare.

And so, bastard feudalism cannot be seen as a cause of the Wars of the Roses in any meaningful way. It neither encouraged nor discouraged rebellion or the flouting of the king's authority on a local or a national level. However, there was always the possibility that a noble might deliberately seek to build up a large armed retinue through the money fee with the firm intention of using force to further his interests. A regional rival might respond likewise: and so a dangerous situation could speedily develop. Ultimately, it was within the king's power to ensure that it did not. There were laws against retaining that could be used, or, if the worse came to the worst and the king decided to intervene personally, then that intervention was usually decisive. However, these sanctions did depend upon the king's prestige and authority. If the country were unfortunate enough to suffer from a weak, irresolute, irresponsible or lazy king, then bastard feudalism might be a useful weapon in the hands of either troublemakers or traitors.

Sub-sections i) and ii) have examined so-called long-term causes of the Wars of the Roses. In fact, these causes complement each other. Bastard feudalism might justly be seen as a symptom of a shift in power from king to nobility that can be identified from the time of Edward III. But it has been suggested that it is easy to over-estimate the importance of these factors. They certainly did not lead in any direct way to war. They did not so weaken kingship that conflict between king and nobility was likely. Indeed, there is no contradiction between a strong nobility and strong kingship - with one absolutely vital proviso. And this is that England had an effective king. As suggested in Chapter 2, the rôle of a king was an extremely demanding one. The changes from Edward III's time probably made it more so. If the kingdom were in the wrong hands, then tensions became crises. Powerful magnates became dangerous magnates. The blood royal became the justification for treasonable plotting. Bastard feudalism became gangsterism or a method of enlisting support for the armies of traitors. And the whole system of interlocking personal loyalties that bound the aristocracy together became fuel for factional confrontation.

b) Short-term Causes

i) The Personality of Henry VI

Given the comments at the end of the previous section, it would seem a good idea to look with particular care at the personality of Henry VI. Chapter 2 demonstrated how the stability of government depended on the king's effectiveness. Indeed, the king's personality touched and affected every facet of power and authority in the kingdom. That personality was so important that it is hard to find an analogy that does justice to it. Perhaps an appropriate one would be to compare a king to the driver of a powerful chariot, pulled by teams of trained but temperamental horses. Without the driver's firm control and discipline, his skill and deftness of touch, his strength of arm, and his sense of direction, the chariot could so easily veer about wildly, spreading destruction and anarchy in its path.

It is a mark of the importance of the king's personality that this section will argue that Henry VI himself was the most important cause of his own downfall. Few kings could meet the criteria of the ideal monarch as outlined in Chapter 1. But few had Henry's tragic and spectacular incompetence.

If Henry was not like a king, it is less easy to be sure what he was like, because the amount of relevant evidence is limited. However, we do have a certain amount of contemporary and near-contemporary comment on his personality. For example, there is the viewpoint from the mid-1460s of an anonymous English chronicler. He is describing the year 1459:

1 In this same time, the realm of England was out of all good
  governance, as it had been many days before, for the king was
  simple and led by covetous counsel, and owed more than he was
  worth ... all the possessions and lordships that pertained to the
5 crown the king had given away, some to lords and some to other
  simple persons, so that he had almost nothing left to own.

Historians have often used the so-called Blacman tract, *A compilation of the meekness and good life of King Henry VI,* as an indication of the king's personality and reputation. There is some dispute over whether John

Blacman, a fellow of Eton College and later a monk, actually wrote the work. Its form is largely that of the reminiscences of a royal chaplain. We can be reasonably sure that it was written in the 1490s in the reign of Henry VII. The tract presents a picture of an unworldly, chaste and devout king and complements perfectly the numbers of miracles allegedly worked by and in the name of the dead king around his tomb. It also complements the efforts being made by Henry VII to persuade the Pope to declare his predecessor a saint. As such, its accuracy must be questionable at best.

> 1 He [Henry VI] was, like a second Job, a man simple and upright, altogether fearing the Lord God, and departing from evil ... a certain reverend prelate of England used to relate that for ten years he held the office of confessor to King Henry; but he declared that
> 5 never throughout that long time had any blemish of mortal sin touched his soul ... This King Henry was chaste and pure from the beginning of his days ... he kept his marriage vow wholly and sincerely, even in the absences of the lady, which were sometimes very long: never dealing unchastely with any other woman ... It
> 10 happened once, that at Christmas time a certain great lord brought before him a dance or show of young ladies with bared bosoms who were to dance in that guise before the king, perhaps ... to entice his youthful mind. But the king was not blind to it, nor unaware of the devilish wile, and very angrily averted his eyes, turned his back
> 15 upon them, and went out to his chamber, saying: "Fy, fy, for shame ...". At another time, riding by Bath ... the king, looking into the baths, saw in them men wholly naked ... At which he was displeased, and went away quickly, abhorring such nudity as a great offence ... I would have you know that he was most eminent
> 20 for that virtue of humility. This pious prince was not ashamed to be a diligent server to a priest celebrating in his presence ... He did so commonly even to me, a poor priest.

In the early sixteenth century, we have the comments of Polydore Vergil. This respected Italian scholar wrote his *Anglica Historia* under commission from Henry VII.

> 1 King Henry [VI] was a man of mild and plain-dealing disposition, who preferred peace before wars, quietness before troubles ... and leisure before business; and, to be short, there was not in this world a more pure, honest and more holy creature. There was in
> 5 him honest shamefacedness, modesty, innocency and perfect patience ...

A more moderate assessment of Henry's religious life would certainly record his piety. It might also draw attention to the surprising amount of time he spent in religious houses later in his reign. However, there was certainly something ostentatious about his piety: witness his extravagant plans for the founding of Eton College and King's College, Cambridge as colleges for priests to mark the ending of his minority. What is particularly significant is the way in which Henry kept changing his mind over the scale of the building at Eton. At one point (in 1449) a full seven years' work had to be demolished to make way for his latest plan. As Bertram Wolffe has pointed out, it is symptomatic of this king's personality that he should choose to mark his accession to power with a massive scheme of religious building. Other kings might prefer the more traditional and knightly course of leading a campaign in France. We might add that the way in which Henry VI wasted huge sums of money through indecision and lack of a steadfast purpose mirrors all too clearly his political life.

It was not as if Henry VI did not have the opportunity to learn the craft of kingship. In his minority, the royal council agonised long and hard over the issue of his education in the military and other kingly virtues. Richard Beauchamp, Earl of Warwick, was appointed Henry's tutor in 1428 when the boy was seven. He provided training in languages, courtesy and a miniature suit of armour. When needed, he imposed some cautious corporal punishment. Warwick was an excellent choice. By November 1437, Henry's minority was at an end and there was little reason to suppose that the 16-year-old would not prove himself to be a king worthy of all the efforts that had gone into his education. The importance of the ending of the minority can scarcely be overstated. The king's council now had no control over Henry. They could certainly advise, remind him of his youth, plead, suggest, point out in the strongest terms - but they could not enforce. Every matter of any importance had to be referred to Henry.

There were early warning signs that the young king's judgment was weak. It is very significant that Henry's early mistakes - which might have been charitably interpreted as the typical errors of a very young man - were repeated time after time throughout his reign. Historian Bertram Wolffe provides a number of examples. On the 11 February 1438, the council clerk was instructed to point out to the king that it was not a good idea to grant pardons to people whose misdemeanours had effectively cost the crown 2,000 marks. And, the very next day, the clerk had to draw Henry's attention to his unwise decision to grant away the office of Constable and Steward of Chirk Castle. This piece of generosity cost the crown 1,000 marks. Even worse, he then sold the castle outright to Henry Beaufort, Bishop of Winchester, who wanted it for his own nephews.

Reckless generosity was not the only problem. In 1441, Henry granted the stewardship of the Duchy of Cornwall to the Earl of Devon. But, in so doing, he showed an absolutely spectacular disregard for his vital role in using patronage to promote decent relations between nobles. He was fully aware of a festering quarrel between one of his own knights, Sir William Bonville, and the earl. Yet Bonville was the sitting steward of Cornwall - and now he was being replaced by his enemy. The council was then left with the unenviable task of sorting out the whole sorry mess.

Why was the king making these kinds of irresponsible mistakes? One reason was that he lacked political skill and awareness. Quite simply, he found it difficult to think through the implications of his decisions. Second, it would appear that he was being manipulated by those closest to him - the men of his household. There is ample evidence to suggest that they quickly developed the skill of tapping the king's lavish patronage. Wardships, castles, crown lands, grants of forfeitures levied on traders breaking customs regulations, mastership of the king's horses, constableships, pensions, apartments at Westminster, even earldoms: and for all this generosity, the king was getting little in return. The problem is that he was making the grants for personal rather than political reasons. As we know, patronage was a vital tool by which the king could spread his own influence through widening his own affinity (or following). An adept king could also use it to balance factions and curb potential local rivalries. In Henry's hands, patronage reduced his influence, worsened factionalism and intensified local rivalries.

The king's long-term influence was lessened because he was depleting his own resources. The most serious aspect of this was the alienation (or granting away) of crown land. This immediately reduced Henry's power. His income inevitably declined, and with it his available patronage. The number of king's retainers was bound to decrease. As we discovered in Chapter 2, the late medieval king was supposed to 'live of his own' except in times of crisis, but reduction in crown lands made it almost impossible for him to run the country on his own income. In this situation, Henry would need to raise money - but how? The commercial classes in London would be reluctant to offer loans to such a spendthrift king, and foreign bankers would be equally unhelpful. The king, in fact, ended up borrowing money from some of his own magnates, which itself reduced his freedom of action and put him further under their influence. Moreover, as we shall see below, he was unable to pay the wages of his nobles who had served the crown in France or on the Scottish border. This made access to the king's undiscriminating favour vitally important. A noble who wanted to benefit from the king's diminishing and wayward patronage had to be at court to see what personal persuasion could do. The extent of the problem caused by the king's extravagant and unreasoning patronage is revealed in the attempts made by the Commons to persuade him to cancel his various grants. An Act of Resumption was passed in the spring of 1450, but Henry made sure that he could insert clauses of exemption. No fewer than 186 clauses were attached to the act. The net result was that the household servants surrendered no more than a third of their gains. Unsurprisingly, in 1451 the Commons made a second attempt, and had the audacity to include a provision whereby the king was to have his grants scrutinised by a committee of councillors. This was an extraordinary attempt to restrict the king's prerogative, and must reflect the despair with which the Commons viewed the financial state of the crown. In fact, any act of resumption was a desperate measure, since it was not only humiliating to the king but also destabilised his relationship with his nobility. Could any noble be sure that a grant received from the king would stand the test of time? The king refused to accept this limitation on his right of patronage, but it has to be said that the second act of resumption was more effective than the first in clawing back crown property.

It is clear that Henry was temperamentally incapable of acting as the fount of justice and the ultimate preserver of law and order. As Chapter 2 suggested, this was indeed a demanding task, given that those entrusted with the upkeep of the laws - the nobles - were the very people who were prepared to exploit them for their own ends if given the chance. Henry VI duly gave them that chance. He effectively sabotaged his own rôle in two ways. First, he was far too ready to offer pardons to those who petitioned for them. To take one instance from many, in 1437 he pardoned seven Devonshire men who had been indicted for the blinding, mutilation and then murder of an employee of the Church. The letter of pardon makes no mention of why the king should have been so lenient. Second, the king allowed the factions he favoured to use the law to further their own interests and those of their affinity. The Paston letters are full of the troubles caused by those who could rely on the protection of men such as the Earl of Suffolk, who had the ear of the king.

The failures in patronage and law and order reflect, of course, Henry VI's wider failure: to build meaningful relationships with all magnates, in which his most powerful subjects felt valued and secure. The next section examines the way in which Richard, Duke of York became increasingly alienated from the court of Henry VI. This discussion will also confirm the assertions made about the king's personality in previous sections. It is particularly important that we examine the Duke of York, since it is York's actions that led directly to the outbreak of armed conflict and the attempt to depose Henry VI.

ii) Richard, Duke of York

A glance at the family tree on page 2 shows that Richard was indeed a magnate of the blood royal. The usurpation of the throne by Henry IV in 1399 had, of course, made royal blood a potentially dangerous commodity should a disaffected magnate possess it (see page 7). In fact, York's father, Richard, Earl of Cambridge, had been executed for a plot against Henry V in support of the rival claims of Edmund, Earl of March (who wanted nothing to do with such treason).

His father's treason did not prevent Richard from inheriting the dukedom of York. By the time Henry VI's minority was at an end in 1437, Richard was also Earl of March and of Ulster. The young magnate's prestige and power led, despite his relative youth and military inexperience, to a year's appointment as lieutenant-general and governor in Lancastrian France.

There was absolutely nothing to suggest in 1437 that York would, in the future, seek to usurp the throne. He had family connections with most of the magnate families - including Henry's favourites the Beauforts - and was anything but a leader of an opposition faction, real or potential. How, then, did this dramatic about-turn take place?

The first reason was financial. Following his first year-long term as lieutenant-general, the English government owed him considerable sums. He was reappointed in 1440: by the time he returned to England in 1445, he was owed an additional and staggering £38,666 - a sum large enough to leave him in serious financial difficulties. Even more serious, however, was the result of Henry VI's favouritism and ill-considered patronage. John Beaufort, Duke of Somerset, was given the government of Gascony and the title of Captain-General of Gascony and France in 1443 in what can only have been seen by York as a snub to his authority as lieutenant-general. Moreover, York must have been feeling more and more isolated from the royal household whose influence over the king seemed to be increasing alarmingly. From the mid-1440s, a faction under William de la Pole, Earl of Suffolk, was monopolising patronage and power. As Ralph Griffiths puts it (see Further Reading, page 159):

1 To those who had no entrée to this favoured circle in the later
  1440s ... it doubtless seemed that Henry was enveloped by an
  impenetrable, self-perpetuating oligarchy that (admittedly) protected him, but yet also isolated him from alternative sources of
5 counsel.

The king's extravagant generosity to these favourites was by this time notorious: and yet, York himself, serving his king in the very difficult circumstances of Lancastrian France, was being forced to borrow money from his friends to make ends meet. On his return from France in 1445, he was not reappointed. His replacement, almost inevitably, was another Beaufort - Edmund, Duke of Somerset, who had succeeded his brother to the dukedom. York was appointed to the lieutenancy of Ireland in 1447, and rightly assumed that this was to get him out of the way. It was 1449 before he could be prevailed upon to take up his appointment. He could see that his own position would be steadily eroded if he went to Ireland. This was particularly galling for a man who was, after the death of Humphrey, Duke of Gloucester in 1447, heir presumptive - i.e. the presumed heir - to the throne. This does not mean that York was in any way keen to encourage the early demise of Henry

VI or the extinction of his line. In fact, York had been a supporter of
Henry VI's marriage with Margaret of Anjou in 1445 and would have
expected children to follow in due course. But York would also expect a
prominent position in the counsels of Henry VI. And he would have
further expected the king to accept and acknowledge his birthright.
However, there were worrying signs that even his status as heir
presumptive was under threat. York's rivals were seeking to influence
the king to consider alternatives to York should Henry's marriage to
Margaret remain childless. Suffolk, as ever, was pulling the strings. He
arranged for his son to marry a Beaufort heiress early in 1450, and the
Beauforts had royal blood in their veins.

It was September 1450 when York returned from Ireland (without
permission). By that time, there had been events of real drama and
tragedy, but the underlying problems from York's point of view had not
changed. There had been a popular rebellion led by Jack Cade (see
pages 44 and 65) which had shaken the government to its foundations.
Suffolk was dead and Normandy was lost (see pages 44 and 63). But the
Duke of Somerset, the very man who had, it seemed, lost Normandy
was back in England, basking once more in the favour of Henry VI and
pulling the strings of government. So, why did York return? We cannot
be sure of his precise motives, but it is likely that he was both furious and
scared. He was furious because he had been replaced by Somerset;
furious that his own property in France had been lost by Somerset's
abject blunderings: but frightened because, like Suffolk before him,
Somerset had a vested interest in destroying Richard of York. And
Henry VI, of course, might well give him the means to do it. Somerset,
after all, was of royal blood: if a case could be manufactured to find York
guilty of treason, there was little to stop Somerset emerging as heir
presumptive.

So, it seems likely that York returned to achieve two things: an
acknowledgement from the king of his status as heir presumptive and
the destruction of Somerset. Only then could he feel secure in his rights.
This interpretation of York's motives fits both his bills of complaint to
Henry justifying his return and also his actions in the May 1451 session
of Parliament, where he sought to capitalise on the situation by getting
one of his own councillors, Thomas Yonge, to propose to the Commons
that York be formally recognised as heir apparent. The Commons
readily agreed, but York found that he had miscalculated the mood of
the peerage and of the king. No magnate supported him, and the king,
stirred to action by the dynastic issue, instantly dissolved Parliament.
For good measure, Yonge was sent to the Tower of London for his
presumption.

The extent of York's anxiety is shown by his extremely risky attempt
in 1452 to achieve his ends by a display of military force. He had made
sure that armed support would be forthcoming from the Earl of Devon
and Lord Cobham, and then issued a personal statement reaffirming his

allegiance to Henry VI but demanding the removal of Somerset. Somerset was accused of plotting to have York disinherited and blamed for the disasters in France. Substantial armies faced each other at Dartford in Kent. York himself was persuaded to negotiate, but, when he went to present his case in person to the king, he found Henry accompanied by none other than Somerset. York was disarmed, taken to London and obliged to swear an oath never again to rebel against the king. Here was unusually determined action from Henry VI. York's failure is a reflection of his own political naivety, the unwillingness of virtually every magnate to contemplate taking up arms against the king and the difficulty faced by rebels who remained essentially loyal to the monarch.

It is not difficult to sympathise with the Duke of York at this point. He is to be seen as largely a victim of Henry VI's failings. The king had allowed himself to become a 'good lord' to Suffolk and Somerset and a correspondingly 'heavy lord' to York. He had shown that he was prepared to see patronage flow in one direction, to ignore the blatant exploitation of the judicial system in the favour of one faction and to permit apparent incompetence to lose English lands in France. In short, York could not trust his king to protect him, let alone grant him the position in royal counsels to which his birth entitled him.

iii) The Insanity of Henry VI: Richard of York as Protector

In August 1453, Henry VI suddenly went mad. The form his madness took was a complete withdrawal from the world. He would not or could not speak or communicate in any way with anyone. Not even the long-hoped for event, the birth of his son in October 1453, penetrated his torpor. He was shown the baby, Edward, and his eyelids flickered - that and no more. Desperate attempts were made to get some response from the king. In March 1454, the Lords tried what numbers and social clout might do, and sent no fewer than 12 representatives. However:

1 they could get no answer ne sign, for no prayer ne desire, lamentable cheer ne exhortation, ne anything that they or any of them could do or say, to their great sorrow and discomfort. And then the Bishop of Winchester said to the King's Highness, that the
5 lords had not dined, but they should go dine them, and wait upon his Highness again after dinner. And so after dinner they come to the King's Highness in the same place where they were before; and there they moved and stirred him, by all the ways and means that they could think, to have answer of the matters aforesaid, but they
10 could have none; and from that place they willed the King's Highness to go into another chamber, and so he was led between two men into the chamber where he lieth.

What had caused this insanity? It is most probable that it was triggered by devastating news: the English had lost Gascony, and the great commander John Talbot, Earl of Shrewsbury, had been killed at the decisive battle of Castillon. More important than its cause were the results of the king's insanity, which lasted up to the Christmas of 1454. Can it be seen as a cause of the Wars of the Roses in any meaningful way?

There is no doubt that it can. First, it is clear that the immediate impact of the king's absence was open violence at a local and regional level. We have already seen that corruption was widespread and that those with the ear of the king were at the heart of intimidation, illegal retaining, embracery and maintenance (see page 54). However, once it became obvious that the king was completely incapacitated and that his uncertain hand was no longer anywhere near the tiller, some magnates took the opportunity to sort out rivalries by full-scale armed conflict. A good example is what happened with the Percys and the Nevilles. In the August of 1453, several hundred Percy retainers ambushed a party of the Nevilles near York. However, it would be pushing the evidence too far to argue that the country slid into civil war as a result of this kind of violence. This is dangerous lawlessness, not a fight for the throne. Of greater significance is the fact that the power vacuum left by the insane king had to be filled. This need led to a struggle between Queen Margaret and the Duke of York that should be seen as a direct cause of the Wars of the Roses, in that it propelled York into claiming the throne.

There is little doubt that the insanity of the king gave York an opportunity. Although, following the birth of Prince Edward, York was no longer heir presumptive, he was nevertheless the magnate closest in blood to the king and would be difficult to exclude from any form of emergency government. In fact, it would be difficult to envisage him in any rôle other than the leading one. But this, of course, would give him the chance to move against Somerset. However, it was not only Somerset who saw York as a threat. The king's madness brought to the fore the queen herself, and she clearly identified York as a danger to her son's succession. In addition, she, like her husband, reposed much trust and affection in Somerset. According to a contemporary letter, she appears to have tried to take upon herself the king's authority:

1 the Queen hath made a bill of five articles, desiring those articles to be granted; whereof the first is that she desireth to have the whole rule of this land; the second is that she may make the Chancellor, the Treasurer, the Privy Seal, and all other officers of this land,
5 with sheriffs and all other officers that the King should make; the third is, that she may give all the bishoprics of this land, and all other benefices belonging to the King's gift; the fourth is that she may have sufficient livelihood assigned her for the King, and the Prince and herself ... as for the fifth article, I can not yet know what
10 it is.

However, there was no precedent for a female regency in England, and the king's council eventually decided on a protectorate on the model of the king's minority. York, as the magnate closest to the throne, was appointed Protector and Defender of the kingdom of England on 27 March 1454. Somerset had been despatched to the Tower in November 1453 as a result of the Duke of Norfolk's accusations of treason over the defeats in France. But York was in no position to destroy Somerset or to control all the workings of government. His tenure of office was uncertain, because it would cease as soon as the king recovered. He was not able to flood the king's household - or those of the queen or the prince - with his own men, because disposing of incumbents would be over-stepping the limits of his authority. He was not even able to prise Calais out of the control of supporters of Somerset. By Christmas 1454, Henry VI had recovered, albeit with no memory of what had happened during the period of his insanity. He declared himself to be in charity with all, and hoped others were of like mind. It did not take him long, however, to have all charges against Somerset dismissed and then to strip York and his adherents (particularly the Nevilles) of their positions of authority. All York's fears resurfaced: the king's charity did not appear to extend to him. As ever, Henry VI lacked an awareness of the implications of his favouritism. An effective - even sensible - king would have made allowances for York's worries. But not Henry. York knew that Somerset would doubtless be looking for revenge. He also knew that the queen's distrust of him had been intensified by their struggle for control of the country during Henry's madness. York was not invited to the council meeting in April at which it was decided to call a Great Council at Leicester (in the Lancastrian power-base of the Midlands), and may well have assumed that this was a prelude to accusations of treason against himself. He and the Nevilles withdrew from court. They did not ask permission.

iv) The Battle of St Albans, May 1455

All York could do was to try what armed force could achieve - the Dartford confrontation all over again. There were the same protestations of loyalty, and the same demands for the removal of 'traitorous' councillors - all ignored by the king. The difference this time was that the sword did what persuasion could not do. In a messy skirmish in St Albans, Somerset and the Earl of Northumberland were killed. Henry was slightly wounded (by accident) and fell into York's hands. Much of the blame for this military defeat must be apportioned to Henry himself. He had - for no obvious reason - suddenly decided to ignore the sensible advice of Somerset (of all people) who wanted the king's forces to set up a fortified position in the face of York's military challenge. Instead, Henry favoured the disastrous advice of Buckingham, who felt that York would not fight. As a result, the Lancastrians were, in all probability, unprepared when York's assault came.

The battle of St Albans scarcely merits the name in military terms, but its political significance was considerable. First, blood had been spilt, and the sons and other relations of Somerset and Northumberland were going to find it very difficult to accept any form of long-term compromise with York. What they wanted was revenge, and the sooner the better. In this way, factionalism was not curbed by Somerset's death: it was made worse. Second, Queen Margaret was now more convinced than ever that only the complete destruction of York would safeguard the succession of her son. There is real doubt over whether Henry VI ever regained his mental health sufficiently to be able to act independently for the rest of his reign. This means that, more than ever, politics meant the struggle to control the king. And the leadership of the Lancastrian party fell upon the shoulders of an uncompromising and ruthless woman, who had every intention of persuading her peace-loving husband to crush the Yorkists once and for all. The importance of this cannot be overstated.

However, it is important to note that York made no claims to the throne, and that Henry was perfectly safe with him. Henry suffered a further breakdown almost immediately, and York was again made Protector.

v) Queen Margaret Takes Control

Early in 1456, the king had recovered sufficiently to make some decisions and, for once, he made an eminently sensible one. Although York was no longer Protector, Henry made sure that his importance was recognised as chief councillor. His Neville ally, the Earl of Warwick, gained entry into Calais as Captain thanks to Henry's support. But this hopeful sign, long overdue, was short-circuited when Henry took refuge inside the queen's castle of Kenilworth, where the defences were immediately strengthened. Against whom? The answer has to be against the Duke of York, despite the fact that York was loyally serving the king's interests in the borders with Scotland. In fact, the government had withdrawn to the Lancastrian heartlands, and officers who had shown a willingness to forge decent relationships between York and the court were replaced by those who were clearly identified as king's - or rather queen's - men. York was summoned to a Great Council at Coventry, and left in no doubt that the queen had been keen to have him arrested. The king was less revengeful, but York and Warwick were both obliged to swear an oath that they would do nothing in future to put in jeopardy the safety of king and kingdom. To be fair to Henry, he made one attempt to reconcile the hatred of the Yorkist and Beaufort factions in a 'love-day' in March 1458 where enemies gave the impression of reconciliation in a solemn procession to St Paul's Cathedral in London. Queen Margaret and Richard of York walked hand in hand. The spectacle was impressive but completely hollow. Bitterness and distrust created by nearly two decades of factional intrigue were not going to fade away by means of a pageant. Contemporary commentators were adamant that the king was increasingly under the control of his queen. The love-day was swept aside as the Lancastrians made further military preparations. Writs were sent out to selected lords, ordering them to appear at Coventry equipped for military service. To anyone with the slightest sympathy for York, this appeared to be nothing more than a trap. Those who failed to appear - York, Warwick, the Earl of Salisbury and Thomas Bourchier, the Archbishop of Canterbury, among others - were then indicted at the queen's insistence. The Yorkists took up arms in the all-too-familiar pattern: still protesting allegiance, still demanding the removal of evil counsellors, and still demanding their rightful place in the king's counsels. Faced with a much larger royal army at Ludford bridge in October 1459, York fled to Ireland, and Warwick, Salisbury and York's son, Edward, Earl of March, to Calais.

A parliament had been summoned to Coventry even before the flight of the Yorkists. In the event, the queen made sure that all York's worse nightmares came true. At this so-called 'Parliament of the Devils' (1459), the decision was taken to attaint York and his adherents: in other words, to 'corrupt their blood' and to disinherit their families once and for all.

In the event, the Yorkists returned to triumph at the battle of Northampton in July 1460. It is vital to note that at this point the victorious York claimed the throne of England. Why now? This is a very difficult question to answer, but it is essential to attempt to do so because the conflicts at this point clearly take on a wider significance. If you wish to define the Wars of the Roses as a set of dynastic conflicts whose target was the throne of England, then your starting date would be 1459. This is a perfectly reasonable approach, although you would have to account for the origins of the conflict. Those origins are not, as we have seen, dynastic. On the other hand, it might be possible to argue that the Duke of York was concealing his ambitions for some years before seizing the appropriate opportunity in 1459. This argument, however, is difficult to substantiate. First, we have no record of what was going on in York's mind. Second, are we really to accept that all York's protestations of loyalty were pure hypocrisy? If he had succeeded in achieving what he saw as his rightful place in the king's counsels and a sense of security for himself and his family, would he really have wanted more? After all, York's actions up to 1459 are responses to perceived threats rather than the plottings of a usurper.

Why, then, the switch from loyal but troubled subject to rival claimant? Certainty and history rarely go together, and so, to offer an explanation, we must be content with an argument based upon probabilities. It makes sense to argue that York had little alternative. He had been pushed into a corner by Henry VI, by Somerset, by Queen Margaret, and every time he escaped he was pushed back in again. The Parliament of the Devils clearly intended to brick him in. He had, after all, seen that victory in battle and the capture of the king had availed him little. What had he to lose?

It is possible that York was expecting support from Warwick in his claim: indeed, it is hardly likely that the matter had not been discussed between them. Section 2 describes the embarrassed response of his adherents and the unworkable compromise patched up whereby Henry VI retained the throne but York was to be his heir. The same section also describes York's death at Sandal and the triumph of his son Edward in taking the throne as Edward IV. The motives of Edward IV are no different from those of his father: his continued struggle is a mere extension of his father's struggles with the added incentive of revenge. We recall that Edward's claim to the throne (such as it was) was buttressed by his allegation that Henry VI had forfeited his right to the throne by failing to honour the Act of Accord with Edward's father. Edward was able to exploit the Londoners' fear of Queen Margaret's northern army and the frequently shaky relationship between the capital and the Lancastrian régime to ensure his proclamation as king in March 1461.

It has been argued that the conflict surrounding the position of the Duke of York is the most important cause of the Wars of the Roses. But this was not stimulated by York's personal ambition so much as the mistakes, weaknesses and insanity of the king. It was the manipulation of the king by his councillors and, in the end, by his wife that pushed York over the brink. This is not to say that York had never considered what the view from the throne must have been like. After all, he was too close to it for it to be likely that he was able to put it out of his mind. But he tried to seize it because the highest place was, in the end, the only safe one. Unfortunately for him, it was left to his son to discover that it could be so.

So far, we have discussed longer-term causes: issues which were part of the nature of late medieval society and which might - in certain circumstances - have created a situation in which civil war was possible. We have also identified shorter-term causes to explain how and when the crisis developed and loomed into view. It has been argued that the most important short-term cause of the outbreak of the Wars of the Roses - indeed, the most important cause of any type - was the personality and mental health of Henry VI. While discussing the shorter-term causes, the situation in which the Duke of York finally sought to overthrow Henry VI has been outlined. This situation - sparked by the conflict with Queen Margaret - may be seen as the *immediate* cause. An alternative way of categorising causes would be to refer to them as either 'direct' or 'indirect' causes. A direct cause would be one which led inexorably to the conflict: an indirect cause might permit other outcomes or be less fundamentally important. Attaching the terms 'direct' and 'indirect' is less straightforward than 'short-term', 'long-term' and 'immediate', but the approach has the merit of forcing the historian to clarify links between causes. At the very least, it stimulates debate. Perhaps the most obvious direct causes of the Wars are those identified as most important above: namely, the personality and insanity of Henry VI, together with the burgeoning hostility between York and the queen. There are, however, other possible short-term causes still to be discussed, and no interpretation would be effective without an examination of them and of their relative importance. Can they be seen as direct or indirect causes?

4 The Ending of the French Wars

Did defeat in Normandy in 1450 lead directly to the Wars of the Roses? After all, it might be possible to argue that England was suddenly flooded with disillusioned veterans who had lost their French lands or sources of booty but not their taste for war. Their resentment and violence might destabilise the country. Also, it might be argued that the shock of defeat was so great that the Lancastrian régime could not recover its prestige.

First of all, we can dismiss the 'bloodthirsty veteran' argument. As Pollard has pointed out, their return was greeted with pity rather than apprehension or fear. However, the 'shock of defeat' argument is much less easy to dismiss. It was inevitable that the régime would be the target of bitter criticism and, since that could not be openly aimed at the king, those councillors held responsible would suffer. And this is precisely what happened at the meeting of Parliament on 6 November 1449. The Norman capital of Rouen had just surrendered, and members of the Commons blamed Suffolk, whose immediate imprisonment they demanded. The allegations are clearly stated in their indictment of the king's favourite. Suffolk, it was said, had encouraged Charles VII ('calling himself king of France') to make war against Henry with the aim, not only of destroying the king's Norman possessions, but also to depose him in favour of Suffolk's own son (having, as we recall, married into the Beaufort family). He was also accused of corrupting the legal system and ignoring it altogether when it suited him. The indictment continued:

1 The said duke ... for covetise of great lucre ... stirred and moved
  your Highness ... ye then being in prosperity and having great
  possessions, to give and grant much part of your said possessions,
  to divers persons in your said realm of England, by the which ye be
5 greatly impoverished ... and so by his subtle counsel, importunate
  and unprofitable labour to your most high and royal estate, the
  revenue of the demesnes and possessions of your crown ... have
  been so amenused and anientised [diminished and destroyed], that
  your commons of this your realm have be so importably charged,
10 that it is nigh to their final destruction.

What saved Suffolk - temporarily - was Henry VI. The king dismissed the charges against him and exiled his friend for five years (for his own protection). Section 2 described his sorry end, when his ship was intercepted and he was beheaded with a sword - and a rusty one at that.

It is significant that the Commons tied in the loss of Normandy with their many other grievances. The loss of Normandy is an indictment of Somerset, of course, but the main responsibility must rest with Henry himself. Henry VI's genuine desire for peace in France (a desire encouraged by his French wife) had led to the handing over of his province of Maine to the French king Charles VII in 1448. From this, Henry VI gained nothing. As a direct result, the king's counsellors were confused and his forces in France disheartened and demoralised. Somerset had the same unrealistic hopes of peace as Henry VI and did as little to discourage Charles VII from the conquest of Normandy. He presided over humiliating surrender after surrender as French troops overran the traditional territories of English France.

As was suggested earlier in the chapter, Henry conspicuously lacked the ability to visualise the wider political implications of his policies. This is not to deny that the effective defence of France was very difficult to fund. It was not easy to get sufficient moneys out of the Commons. But it was almost impossible to do so when the Commons had lost confidence in the king's ability to use it effectively. It was all too likely to end up in the pockets of Henry's favourites.

Nevertheless, the fall of Normandy did not destroy the Lancastrian government. It may well have sparked off the Cade rebellion (see Section 5) but, as has been suggested earlier, the régime recovered. In 1451 and 1452, Henry showed unusual vigour and commitment - even to law and order. For the first time in his reign, he undertook judicial progresses and took part in the sitting in judgement over rebels. There were, as we have seen, temporary successes in France under the Earl of Shrewsbury and York's weak position was relentlessly exposed by the Dartford incident. The final loss of Gascony in 1453 was not greeted with the same wailing and gnashing of teeth as had greeted the loss of Normandy. All in all, then, we can reject the argument that the loss of Normandy and Gascony can be seen as a direct cause of the Wars of the Roses. The defeat was most significant as an indirect cause in the sense that it provided the Duke of York with further justification for his attacks on Henry's councillors and, indeed, had stimulated his hatred of Somerset himself. But, as has been noted, it did not need the French defeats to convince York that his dynasty was in danger. It is York's perception of that danger that most directly caused the Wars.

5 The Cade Rebellion, 1450

The rising took place in Kent, Surrey, Middlesex and parts of Sussex in response to threats made by the Sheriff of Kent and Sussex that Kent would be turned into a deerpark because of the alleged involvement of Kentishmen in the death of the Duke of Suffolk. But, of course, the causes were more deep-rooted than this, as is suggested by the fact that the rebels came from all social classes (except the magnates). As was described in section 2, they did not regard themselves as disloyal, but instead wished to remove from the king those councillors and members of the royal household who, they alleged, had impoverished the crown, corrupted the judicial system and lost Normandy. The leader, Jack Cade, made various claims to being of royal blood, but the intention was never to depose Henry VI. The rebel forces duly backed off when it appeared that Henry was to take the field against them in person, although they cheerfully killed household men when part of the royal army went in pursuit of them. Typically, Henry then failed to show the courage necessary to encounter the rebels personally: he withdrew to the Midlands, so abandoning London to the rebels. Cade executed the Treasurer of England, Lord Saye, and William Cromer, a sheriff of Kent, for their alleged corruption and particular misdeeds in Kent itself. The rebels left London and dispersed only after a fierce battle with the garrison of the Tower (abetted by some Londoners) and the offer of royal pardons. Cade was later captured and killed.

The rebellion is significant in that it demonstrates once again the depth of discontent with the corruption and failings of the faction-led Lancastrian government. It also demonstrates Henry VI's inordinate capacity for misjudgment and a possible lack of physical courage. Cade's rebellion, therefore, reflects underlying factors that led to the Wars of the Roses, but it is not possible to see it as either a direct or an indirect cause in itself.

6 Conclusion

When his minority ended, the young Henry VI undoubtedly faced many challenges. As King of France, his was a difficult inheritance to maintain. His father, Henry V, had done the relatively simple thing and conquered territory: his early death relieved him of the ticklish task of actually administering it. Nevertheless, Henry's inheritance had survived the long minority - so it was possible to defend it. Admittedly, it required the full support of the political nation to fund the necessary defences and military campaigns. And the king would probably need to fulfil his traditional rôle by leading armies into battle. There were other challenges. Certainly, the power of the upper nobility had been increasing for generations. The king would need to harness that power to his own needs. But then, it was the job of a king to meet such challenges. It was not an impossible task. If it had been, one would see the decline of monarchy in England throughout the fifteenth and sixteenth centuries. This simply did not happen. As we shall see, both Edward IV and Henry VII were able to overcome many of their problems and to secure - for themselves at least - an enhanced authority and a reasonably stable realm.

And so, the so-called long-term causes of the war are not really causes at all. At the very most, they might be seen as 'potential' causes. The increase in the power of the nobility and bastard feudalism were destabilising only if a weak king were unable to control them for his own ends. However, if the king's relationship with significant sections of the nobility were to break down, then some form of conflict was likely. It was Henry VI's misfortune that he was king. His personality was so inappropriate to his rôle that he made virtually every conceivable mistake. He lacked the political awareness to balance factions. He could not restrain his own generosity, or recognise its implications. He ignored the king's military function, and made peace the goal of his policy in France without identifying the means by which it might be achieved. He was easily influenced by councillors and by his wife. He failed to supervise the judicial system, and allowed it to be exploited by the powerful to further their own interests.

The York incident at Dartford and the Cade rebellion show that discontent caused largely by the king's behaviour could easily turn into some form of military conflict. The deaths of Somerset and Northumberland at St Albans added fuel to the flames, since bloodshed made it very unlikely that important magnate families would be reconciled. But it was the king's insanity that turned chronic and sometimes violent instability into a dynastic struggle: not because the king was mad, but because the power vacuum brought out and greatly intensified the clash between the Duke of York and Queen Margaret. The queen identified York as the threat to her son's inheritance, and therefore used all means she could to destroy him once and for all. York, faced with the awareness that his family could be erased from the political map of England, sought the throne as his only guarantee of security.

Making notes on 'The Downfall of Henry VI'

Now is the time for careful and detailed note-making. As you do so, remember that the chapter is seeking to answer the question 'What were the causes of the outbreak of the Wars of the Roses (up to 1461)?' The detail you select must always provide you with evidence for or against a particular line of argument. This explains why the headings below (and in the chapter itself) are frequently couched as questions.

1   Introduction. Notes as such are not needed on this brief section, but make sure that you understand the reasoning behind the content of Chapters 3 and 4.

2.   A narrative of events. The information here is best presented in a time-line (say from 1431 to 1461).

3.   Causes of the downfall of Henry VI. No notes, but be sure that you
     understand what is meant by 'long-term' and 'short-term' causes,
     and also 'hierarchy of factors'.
     Long-term causes
3.1 Had there been a long-term shift in power from the king to the
     nobility?
3.2 How important was bastard feudalism as a cause of the Wars of the
     Roses?
3.3 What are the links between the long-term shift in power and bastard
     feudalism?
     Short-term causes
3.4 How important a factor was the personality of Henry VI? You
     might find it helpful to conclude your notes on this section by
     comparing the qualities of the ideal king outlined in Chapter 2 with
     Henry's failings.
3.5 Richard, Duke of York. Was there anything in Richard's back-
     ground that would predispose him to challenge Henry VI? What
     were the reasons for his growing discontent with his position? Was
     that discontent justified? Why did he resort to force at Dartford?
3.6 The insanity of Henry VI: Richard of York as Protector. What was
     the nature of the king's insanity? What was its immediate effect in
     terms of law and order? Why did the queen attempt to become
     regent? What did York do as Protector? What were Henry's actions
     on the recovery of his wits?
3.7 The battle of St Albans. What factors led to the battle of St Albans?
     What was the result?
3.8 Queen Margaret takes control. What steps did the queen take
     against York, and why? Why and under what circumstances did
     York make his first open bid for the throne?
4.   The ending of the French Wars. How important were the defeats in
     Normandy and Gascony as causes of the Wars?
5.   The Cade Rebellion, 1450. If the rebellion cannot be seen as a
     cause of the Wars as such, what is its significance?
6.   Conclusion. I would strongly advise the use of a spider-diagram to
     deal with the conclusion. Most readers will know how these work,
     but a few words of advice may be helpful. The body of the spider is
     the main question or topic: in this case, the causes of the downfall of
     Henry VI (to 1461). The legs of the spider are the main themes
     within the topic: in this case, the various causes. These legs then
     have feet, which are the detail making up the themes. The great
     advantage of spider-diagrams is that they display the links between
     information (the legs and the feet, of course). The summary below
     provides an example of the legs. I suggest you complete the feet.

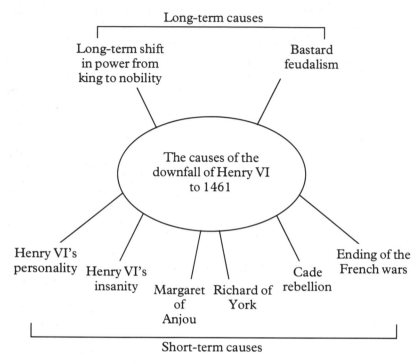

Summary - The Downfall of Henry VI

Answering essay questions on 'The Downfall of Henry VI'

It is conceivable that an examiner might set a question purely on the period covered by this chapter, although it is more likely that a broader time-scale would be used. A question might ask for a discussion of the causes of the conflicts from their outbreak to the death of Henry VI (1471), to the usurpation of Richard III (1483), or to the death of Richard III and the usurpation of Henry VII in 1485. They might even go as far as the battle of Stoke (1487); a remoter possibility (but still a possibility) is the capture of Warbeck in 1497. The broader scale allows candidates to compare causes. You must certainly know these dates! Nevertheless, we should at least consider possible questions for the period c.1450 to 1461. Here are some examples.

1   'The outbreak of the Wars of the Roses up to the usurpation of the throne by Edward of York was caused largely by instability within society itself.' Comment on this view.
2   How far was the personality of Henry VI responsible for his deposition in 1461?

3   To what extent was an over-mighty nobility responsible for the outbreak of the Wars of the Roses, up to c.1461?
4   Why was Edward of York able to overthrow Henry VI in 1461?

It should be clear that you are not going to get a question 'What were the causes of the Wars of the Roses?' After all, this would simply invite a list and would require little skill apart from a facility with the English language and a decent memory. A good essay is, above all, an argument. Each of the above essays demands a clear line of argument as the answer. You might like to consider which is the most difficult, and why.

Hopefully, to answer that question, you will have looked very carefully at the precise wording. Many of you will have been told to IDENTIFY KEY WORDS as the first step. This is good advice - particularly for the more complex or more wordy questions, where you might miss the point. Try it for the examples above.

Question 4 might seem the most straightforward. The only real danger is to miss the date and try to discuss issues leading to the Warwick rebellions or the readeption (as described in Chapter 4). But you must make sure, when discussing causes, that you are prepared to offer a explanation of which cause or causes are to be seen as the most important. For example, no examiner would be impressed by a mere list as an answer to question 4. If you have spotted the key words 'To what extent' and 'How far' in other questions, then at least you will have realised that a list will not work.

Question 1 is what might be called a 'challenging statement' type of question. Some students find these difficult. The best approach is to state your argument clearly in your introduction. If you wish, you could use the opening words 'I intend to argue' to start yourself off. It may seem quite mechanical, but at least it forces you to argue a case. And that, as we have seen, is the key to a good essay. Try writing introductions for the essays above.

Source-based questions on 'The Downfall of Henry VI'

1 Sources on the personality of Henry VI
Carefully read the extracts from the so-called Blacman tract and the *Anglica Historia* of Polydore Vergil on page 51. Answer the following questions.
a)   What picture of Henry VI is presented by the two sources? (4 marks)
b)   Of the two writers, which seems to favour the king most? Explain your answer. (3 marks)
c)   'The sources may be unreliable, but they nonetheless have a real value for the historian.' How far do you agree, with reference to Blacman and Vergil? (8 marks)

CHAPTER 4

The Downfall of the Yorkist Kings and the End of the Wars of the Roses

1 Introduction

Chapter 3 ended with the usurpation of the throne by Edward of York in 1461. A straightforward narrative of the subsequent conflicts in the reigns of Edward IV, Richard III and Henry VII was provided in Chapter 1 (see pages 10-11). It might be useful to re-read that section now.

The purpose of this chapter is to examine those problems facing the monarchs which led to political conflict. As in Chapter 3, our main interest is in the causes of the conflicts. The classification of causes used in Chapter 3 - long-term, short-term, immediate, direct, and indirect - will prove useful as we seek to identify and then to compare the causes of the conflicts from reign to reign.

Comparing conflicts in this way is not easy. It might, therefore, be helpful to outline the basic argument of the chapter. But it needs to be emphasised that what follows is the author's interpretation and as such is certainly open to challenge. Generally speaking, of course, a writer wants to convince his or her readers of the validity of the view presented. This means that the information provided will be selected and used to support that interpretation. Those readers relatively new to the study of history might like to bear in mind a few suggestions for evaluating an interpretation: suggestions which are also useful to consider when writing essays. First, are the arguments clear? Second, are supporting evidence and examples used convincingly? Third, is the writer prepared to admit where there are possible alternative views and/or where sources do not permit a firm conclusion?

And so to the outline of the argument. The early years of Edward IV's reign were characterised by dissent and rebellion. These were in part caused by Lancastrian resistance to the new dynasty and in part by the legacy of aristocratic violence from Henry VI's time. But the most important cause was the personal ambition and resentment of the over-mighty Earl of Warwick. However, Warwick is not to be seen in any way as a typical noble, and his rebellion is therefore not to be taken as the result of a long-term shift in power from king to nobility. His over-mightiness was the product of a particular set of circumstances: namely, the fact that he had been the chief supporter of the House of York in its attempts to usurp the throne and had been rewarded as such. Following the defeat of Warwick and the Lancastrians in 1471, Edward IV presided over a relatively stable kingdom. This is significant because it suggests that society itself was not inherently self-destructive. It also suggests that a strong king could indeed control powerful nobles. Nevertheless, there were serious tensions within the magnate class and within the royal family itself which Edward had been able to control but which surfaced after his premature death. These tensions focussed on the fraught relationship between the king's brother Richard of Gloucester and the Woodville family of the queen. The fact that Edward IV's sons had been brought up to identify with the Woodvilles was a further stimulus to Gloucester's *coup d'état* of 1483. But it was primarily a ruthless personal ambition that led to Gloucester's usurpation of the throne. There are similarities between Warwick and Gloucester's actions - both were resentful of the position of the Woodvilles, for example - but their ambitions were different and so were the circumstances which fuelled them. Once again, we should be suspicious of arguments that allege a long-term instability in English society as the prime cause of the conflicts. The crises within Richard III's reign reflect the suspicion and anger with which his usurpation was greeted. However, his death in battle was the result of a military blunder. And finally, the last conflicts of the Wars of the Roses in the reign of Henry VII are essentially dynastic: the attempt to exploit the king's relatively weak claim to the throne by putting forward Yorkist pretenders. After the defeat of the pretenders Simnel and Warbeck, Henry succeeded in controlling and manipulating his nobility. The days of the over-mighty noble were gone. Over-mighty nobles were the product of the specific failures of kings: their demise, the product of the specific successes of other kings.

2 The Reign of Edward IV, 1461-71: Problems Facing the New King

a) The Long-term Problem of the Power of the Nobility

In Chapter 3, we identified a long-term shift in power from king to nobility which was a challenge an effective king would need to meet. But we also argued that a stronger nobility did not necessarily imply a weaker king if that increased strength were channelled in the king's interest. However, the problem for Edward IV was undoubtedly increased as a result of the turmoil in Henry VI's reign. The nobility had seen that violence and revolt could be a useful tool in both local and national conflicts. Edward himself had only to reflect on his own fortunes to see that this was true. His own family had used armed insurrection as an attempt - at first - to recover what they saw as their rightful place in the counsels of the king. And, in the end, the son of an outcast noble was now King of England as a direct result of rebellion. On top of this, the fighting had left a trail of bloodshed and of old scores to settle. It would, perhaps, be overstating the case to suggest that a discontented noble would now immediately reach for his sword. But, as a result of the outbreak of the Wars of the Roses, that sword was certainly kept close at hand and might be raised against the king. Subsequent sections will allow us to assess the extent of this problem and also of Edward's success or otherwise in handling it.

b) An Immediate Problem: the Defeated Lancastrian Nobility

Although the Lancastrians had been defeated at Towton, (see page 46), their cause was anything but dead. With help from the Scots, French or both, they might hope to reverse the fortunes of war. By 1465, Henry VI had been captured in Lancashire, but this made little difference. What mattered was Edward, Henry's son and heir, and, by this time, he was safe in France. Here, then, was a potent focus for the would-be rebel, be he die-hard Lancastrian or noble dissatisfied with his lot under the first Yorkist king. The Lancastrian cause was also a useful weapon in the hands of any ruler who wished to embarrass the king of England. Edward IV's foreign policy had to take into account the need both to legitimise his dynasty in the eyes of his fellow monarchs and also to prevent them from assisting with a Lancastrian invasion of his kingdom (see pages 134-5).

What, then, should the king do with the Lancastrian supporters among the nobility? If he were unable to secure the loyalty of at least some of them, then he would be forced to rely on a small group of Yorkist nobles to control the country. This would be dangerously close to government by faction. Sensibly enough, Edward made every effort to attract Henry VI's foremost allies to his service. Rather than seek revenge, he was liberal with pardons. Even the Beauforts - long-time rivals and enemies of the house of York - were offered a tempting mixture of forgiveness and reward. To Henry Beaufort, Duke of Somerset, Edward proffered his personal friendship. Somerset accompanied the king on hunts, shared the royal chamber and was rewarded with a tournament held in his honour. In 1463, his title, lands and castles were restored to him. Edward also provided some ready cash to tide him over as he returned to his former status. However, the extent of Somerset's gratitude was made clear within the year. He took part in a rebellion in Northumbria, fell into the hands of the Nevilles, and was executed in 1464.

Beaufort's *volte-face* was one of many. For instance, the staunch Lancastrian Sir Ralph Percy surrendered the Northumbrian fortress of Dunstanburgh to the Yorkists in the autumn of 1461. Instead of replacing him by a Yorkist, Edward allowed Percy to retain his command. In October of the next year, Percy extended his welcome to an expeditionary force under Margaret of Anjou. The Lancastrians withdrew, but Percy was, incredibly enough, forgiven again and left in charge with the opportunity to repeat his treachery. He duly obliged when, in March 1463, he opened his gates to the king's enemies in defiance of Edward's interests and commands. It had been worth trying, but it has to be said that Edward's attempt to conciliate the former Lancastrians was unsuccessful. Perhaps he was being unduly optimistic. He was asking men to ignore sworn and almost instinctive allegiance to a king in whose quarrel members of their own families had perished. In return, they would receive reward from an interloper whose success was by no means certain. It is a characteristic of Edward that he should rely too much on the persuasive power of his own attractive personality in his relations with the nobility.

In the face of this persistent failure of his policy, Edward was essentially forced to rely on that narrow power-base of his trusted Yorkist supporters. This would, in turn, expose the difficulties inherent in the position of Richard Neville, Earl of Warwick. The following sections look closely at Warwick, because his career under Edward IV highlights the longer-term problem of instability focussed on the 'over-mighty noble'. It also sheds further light on the king's personality and his policy on patronage.

c) The Problem of Warwick

Warwick might be kingmaker, but what does a kingmaker do when the king is made? Making kings can hardly become a habit or a hobby. Warwick would expect Edward IV to recognise his contribution by suitably generous patronage, and this is exactly what happened. Captain of Calais, Constable of Dover castle, chief steward of many of the lands of the Duchy of Lancaster, Admiral of England, lordships in the northern and Welsh Marches - enough, one might think, even for a kingmaker. But it was not enough for Warwick. Contemporary sources and subsequent commentators agree that Warwick's greed was boundless. What made him potentially dangerous was his desire to preserve an ascendancy over the king that could not be challenged. To do this, he would need to prevent the possibility of rivals (singly or in factions) building up a large enough power-base in either land or in the king's counsels to threaten his absolute pre-eminence.

No effective king could allow Warwick to assume such a position. Edward IV had every intention of being an effective king. He was generous by nature, but was prepared, even in his early, inexperienced years, to build up the power of nobles other than Warwick in the interests of the security of the crown. Charles Ross has concluded that the king's use of patronage was astute, and that it was indeed in part intended to offset the power of the over-mighty Warwick. This seems a fair assessment. The attempted conciliation of the Lancastrians had been worth trying. But the main thrust of Edward's policy was sensible and much more successful. He placed men who owed their advancement to his favour alone with the task of establishing royal control over large areas of the country. William, Lord Hastings and

William, Lord Herbert are the best examples. Hastings was of solid gentry stock from a family conspicuous for its loyalty to the Dukes of York. He was the king's chamberlain by 1461. In charge of Edward's personal suite of rooms in the royal palaces, he had intimate access to the king and was widely regarded as the man whose advice the king most heeded. He was established as Edward's lieutenant in the east Midlands - an area with strong Lancastrian sympathies. Significantly, Hastings replaced Warwick as steward of Duchy of Lancaster property in the area. Sir William Herbert, as he then was, had been sheriff in Glamorgan and a steward to the Duke of York in various lordships in the Welsh Marches. He had proved his loyalty to the House of York in battle, and was elevated to the magnate class when Edward decided to make him his principal lieutenant in the potential trouble-spot of South Wales. In so doing, the king overrode the ambitions of Warwick by rescinding grants made to the earl in that area and handing them over to Herbert. In 1468, Herbert was made Earl of Pembroke.

No doubt Warwick was less than pleased at the influence and increasing power of Herbert and Hastings, which he must have guessed was in part designed to offset his own. But he must have been deeply shocked when he heard about the king's impetuous and secret marriage in 1464 with the widow Elizabeth Woodville. There is absolutely no reason to see the marriage itself as the result of cool political calculation on the part of the king. Its origin lay in the strength of his sexual desire for Elizabeth Woodville. However, we shall see that the marriage had crucial short and long-term implications for the king's relations with Warwick and the rest of the nobility.

3 The Woodville Marriage

It was important for the new king to marry reasonably promptly and to marry well. Apart from providing the hoped-for son to succeed him, a prestigious marriage into a European royal family would legitimise his dynasty on the international stage. All this Edward knew. But, as was suggested in the previous section, the king's motives for marrying Elizabeth Woodville had more to do with her sexual attractions than with her political standing. Contemporary opinion was divided on her attractiveness but united on her political standing. Of the latter, she had very little. Her first husband, Sir John Grey, had been killed at the battle of St Albans - fighting on the Lancastrian side. She cannot be seen as belonging to the higher nobility. Her mother was a French aristocrat of status, but her father was no more than a respectable member of the gentry. She was also overburdened with relatives: two sons by the previous marriage, no fewer than seven sisters - all unmarried - and five brothers. Edward's instant new family was likely to be expensive. As relatives of a queen, they would all expect a spectacular rise in their fortunes.

Small wonder, then, that Edward kept his marriage secret until the last possible moment. Not even Hastings seems to have known about it. As for Warwick, he was blithely hoping for a marriage for Edward with a member of the royal family of France. Edward finally let fall the bombshell in the September of 1464. Warwick, along with the other magnates, must have been alarmed at Edward's lack of judgment. It was also a clear indication that he held no special place in the king's counsels or affections.

What of the short-term impact of the Woodville marriage (i.e. within the reign of Edward IV)? First of all, it is not the case, as some historians have argued, that the Woodvilles were able to manipulate royal patronage and that others were excluded from Edward's favour. Nor did Edward impoverish the crown to promote his in-laws. He was by no means over-generous to the Woodvilles. The only real exception is the queen's father, who was made Treasurer of England and created Earl Rivers in 1466. A year later, he was Constable of England. These offices were lucrative, but Rivers received not one grant of land. His son, Anthony, Lord Scales, received the useful but relatively minor grant of the Isle of Wight but little else until his father's death. Nor was the queen herself deluged with gifts or the means to run an extravagant household. However, it would cost Edward nothing financially to manipulate the aristocratic marriage market in the Woodville interest. He made sure that the Woodvilles married into the most wealthy or prestigious noble families. One anonymous chronicler makes it clear why Warwick at least had reason to be resentful of the special offers no one could refuse.

1 In the month of January, Catherine, Duchess of Norfolk, a slip of a
girl of about eighty years old, was married to John Woodville, the
queen's brother, aged twenty years; a diabolical marriage ... The
king caused Henry, Duke of Buckingham, to marry a sister of
5 Queen Elizabeth to the secret displeasure of the Earl of Warwick.
And the son and heir of the Earl of Essex married ... another sister
of the queen ... In September a marriage was made at Windsor
between the son and heir of Lord Herbert and Mary, sister of
Queen Elizabeth ... And the lord king knighted Herbert's heir and
10 created him Lord Dunster, to the secret displeasure of the Earl of
Warwick and the magnates of the land ... In the month of October
at Greenwich the king arranged a wedding between Thomas Grey,
knight, the queen's son, and Lady Anne, heiress of the Duke of
Exeter, the king's niece, to the great and secret displeasure of the
15 Earl of Warwick, for a marriage was previously bespoken between
the said Lady Anne and the son of the Earl of Northumberland, the
Earl of Warwick's brother ...

Warwick himself had two daughters. Under normal circumstances they would marry into the great families with royal blood. The most obvious candidate was the very Duke of Buckingham who had been presented with a Woodville in place of a Neville. According to the report of Dominic Mancini, Buckingham was less than happy with the bargain:

> ... he had been forced to marry the queen's sister, whom he scorned to wed on account of her humble origin.

Buckingham and Warwick, then, had little reason to be pleased with the Woodvilles' near-monopoly on aristocratic marriages. But for other magnates, it was an opportunity rather than a barrier. A rising noble such as Herbert could see his new status confirmed and enhanced by a marriage alliance with the king's instant new family. Nevertheless, the evidence suggests that the Woodvilles became very unpopular very quickly. There are two main reasons for this. First, the rapidity and scale of their social climbing was resented by the long-established nobility. Second, they seem to have been more than usually objectionable. With honourable exceptions - Sir Anthony Woodville, perhaps - the Woodville clan appears to have been arrogant, grasping and vengeful. One chronicler, Robert Fabyan, describes what happened when they developed a grudge against Sir Thomas Cook, a former Lord Mayor of London. Their methods included ransacking Cook's property and attempting to pack juries to get him condemned for treason.

Warwick's antipathy to the Woodvilles was shared by the king's two brothers - George, Duke of Clarence, and Richard, Duke of Gloucester. As a general rule, brothers were at best a misfortune to a king. Prone to envy and jealousy, they were a little too inclined to imagine themselves in their elder's place, doing a far better job. Clarence was very much of this type. He was charming, eloquent, handsome, vindictive, jealous, unreasonable and, in short, the perfect tool for a discontented and arrogant man like the Earl of Warwick. If the earl could secure the marriage of Clarence to his daughter Isabel, then Clarence's interests would be bound up with those of his father-in-law. Given that the Woodvilles had cornered the marriage market, it is understandable that Warwick should contemplate this union: and also understandable that it should be vetoed by the king. Up to the birth of his son, Edward, in 1470, the heir presumptive was, of course, Clarence. Edward had no wish to see his unreliable brother united to the family of the resentful kingmaker. Nevertheless, Warwick took the trouble to negotiate secretly for the necessary permission from the Pope for the prospective marriage to take place. Since Isabel and Clarence were closely related, papal dispensation was needed.

4 Warwick in Rebellion, July-October 1469

On 11 July 1469, the marriage of Isabel and Clarence took place in Calais, taking advantage of the king's preoccupation with a series of risings in the north led by 'Robin of Redesdale'. Robin was probably Sir John Conyers, who just happened to be a cousin of Warwick. The Warkworth chronicle explicitly states that the rebellion took place at the instigation of the Warwick faction. Edward's response to the rebellion was far too slow. He seems to have found it difficult to believe that Warwick and Clarence could engage in treason. The king was ill-prepared and out-of-touch with what was going on. A royal army was defeated by Warwick's forces at Edgecote on 26 July. The stunned king was captured three days later by the Archbishop of York (brother of Warwick) and treated as courteously as it is possible to treat a prisoner. Warwick then took the opportunity to execute as many of the Woodvilles and their allies as he could lay his hands on. Earl Rivers, Sir John Woodville and the Earl of Pembroke were duly beheaded. Their offence was to have stood in the way of what Warwick saw as his own rightful dominance.

But now what? Warwick held the king, but not the reins of power. He had no right to act as king. He does not seem to have thought seriously of replacing Edward with Clarence at this stage, and certainly would have had no justification for so doing. Into this power vacuum leapt some riotous Londoners, a number of violent nobles bent on sorting out some local disputes and - more importantly - a pro-Lancastrian rebellion in the north. Warwick simply could not raise troops without the king's authority, and had little choice but to release Edward. The rebellion was crushed, and the king resumed his authority without - sensibly - trying to destroy Warwick or Clarence. There followed an uneasy truce. Warwick had executed some of his Woodville adversaries, but had not established his dominance.

Why had Warwick resorted to rebellion? There are a number of possible explanations. One argument would seek to blame Edward IV for provoking the earl by deliberately seeking to neutralise his power through building up the Woodvilles as an opposing faction. This view can be dismissed. In the first place, Edward had no intention of dismantling Warwick's position. It was far too useful to him. He naturally wished to build up other power-blocs as part of effective kingship and to avoid over-reliance on one man. But these were not set up to rival or to destroy Warwick: simply to place him within a power-structure rather than allow him to dominate it completely. After all, Edward's generosity to Warwick continued up to the time of his rebellion in the form of various grants of land, stewardships, wardships and profits from the king's mines. Second, the Woodvilles were not given sufficient land - the real source of power - for them to be seen as rivals to Warwick's position. As Rosemary Horrox has argued, the Woodvilles' influence did not derive so much from land as from their office-holding. As a result, their personal following was less substantial than many historians have assumed. Of course, it is understandable that Warwick should be affronted by the way in which the Woodvilles controlled the marriage market, and his sense of pride and status doubtless made him look down on them as upstarts. His pride was also dented by the way in which the king pursued the Woodvilles' preferred pro-Burgundian line in foreign policy despite Warwick's personal commitment to a pro-French line. It is also true that Edward IV appears to have enjoyed irritating Warwick's brother George Neville, Archbishop of York, who had been dismissed from his position as Chancellor in 1467. But, in the end, these are only reasonable grounds for discontent. They are not sufficient to explain Warwick's rebellion, unless we add the vital factor - the profoundly unreasonable personality of Warwick. He chose to forget that no king worth the name could allow himself to be dominated by the wishes of one man. He should have realised that this was a lesson Henry VI had failed to learn to his cost. And Warwick should have reflected on the fates of Suffolk and Richard of York. Warwick was a devious and a cunning man, but his political sense was obscured by his pride and ambition. He had no clear aims and objectives that could appeal to other nobles. Apart from Clarence and the Neville affinity, he lacked magnate support. In his first rebellion, he relied upon the old claim that he was simply removing evil counsellors from the king's presence. He was also able to exploit what appears to be some genuine popular dissatisfaction with the Yorkist king. But any further rebellion would be exposed for what it was - personal ambition.

5 Warwick's Second Rebellion, March 1470

Warwick's first rebellion had failed to achieve his aim of securing a position of unchallengeable dominance over the king and country. But he was not the man to learn from his mistakes. His ambition was simply incompatible with kingship itself. Having failed with Edward, he clearly felt that Clarence might be easier to manipulate - although there is no evidence that he would prove any more manageable than Edward himself. Clarence was eager enough to try his luck against his brother again. Warwick and Clarence therefore took the opportunity of disturbances in Lincolnshire in March 1470 to take up arms against Edward. The trouble in Lincolnshire started as a local feud that developed into a full-scale rebellion once it became clear that the king intended to intervene with force. Rumours spread that Edward was out to seek revenge against the Lincolnshire men who had opposed him in past conflicts. Warwick and Clarence were in contact with the rebels, but the king's swift military action dispersed the Lincolnshire men near Stamford. The site of the rout became known as Lose-coat field because the defeated rebels threw off clothing to make a suitably rapid get-away. The official account of the battle - the *Chronicle of the Rebellion in Lincolnshire* - describes how the rebel soldiers included men in Clarence's livery. News of the defeat disrupted attempts by Warwick to raise men in the north and Clarence to do likewise in the west. The tone of Edward's letters to the pair of them changed from conciliatory to menacing, and they decided that France looked a safer haven than the royal court. Warwick and Clarence were unable to gain access to Calais, and so ended up at the court of the French king, Louis XI.

This was a useful place to be. Louis was prepared to consider helping with an invasion of England because Edward IV had sided with the French king's enemy, the Duke of Burgundy. But a rather embarrassing meeting had to be arranged first: Warwick was to face Margaret of Anjou. His only realistic chance of recovering his estates and influence was to assist with the restoration of Henry VI. In other words, the headstrong and arrogant Warwick had to make some sort of alliance with the headstrong and arrogant queen whose exile had been brought about largely through his efforts. And, in the background, was the headstrong and arrogant Duke of Clarence, the usurper's brother. In the end, Warwick agreed to help with the restoration and Margaret offered a grudging forgiveness which was sealed by a marriage treaty. On 25 July 1470, Edward, Prince of Wales and Warwick's younger daughter, Anne, were betrothed. Something of the tension of the negotiations is admirably captured by an unknown writer of the time:

> 1 the said queen was right difficile, and showed to the King of France
> ... that with the honour of her and her son, he ne she might not, nor
> could not pardon the said earl, which hath been the greatest causes
> of the fall of King Henry ... The Earl of Warwick, all these things
> 5 heard, said unto the queen that he confessed well that by his
> conduct and mean that the King Henry and she were put out of the
> realm of England; but, for an excuse and justification thereof, he
> shewed that the King Henry and she by their false counsel had
> enterprised the destruction of him and his friends in body and in
> 10 goods, which he never had deserved against them ... Also he said
> over that, and well confessed that he was causer of the upsetting of
> the King of England that now is, but now, seeing the evil terms that
> the king hath kept him ... now he will be as far contrary and enemy
> unto him hereafter ...

However reluctant or tense the alliance might have been, in military terms it was remarkably successful. Faced with a rising among the Nevilles in the north, Edward IV moved to crush them in the knowledge that he was taking a risk whatever he did. If he ignored the rebellion to safeguard the south against invasion from France, his danger would be great. If he ignored the south to crush the rebellion, his danger would be equally great. It is all too easy to say that he made the wrong decision in dealing with the north: but it certainly gave Warwick and Clarence the chance to land in the west country in September 1470. In fact, it looks rather as if the Neville rising was intended to distract the king. If so, the ploy worked. Warwick was certainly lucky that his invasion fleet had taken advantage of favourable winds, and lucky that Edward delayed unnecessarily in York after the Neville rebellion melted away. On discovering that Lord Montagu had deserted to join his brother Warwick and was bearing down fast on his own inadequate forces, Edward made the hastiest of escapes from King's Lynn to the Netherlands and so to Charles of Burgundy, his brother-in-law. Charles, it has to be said, was not unduly welcoming. He was too concerned about possible alliances between a Lancastrian England and France against himself to offer military assistance to Edward.

6 The Readeption and Edward IV's Recovery of the Throne

The Readeption is the legal term used to describe the restoration of Henry VI to the throne on 3 October 1470. In one sense, there never was a readeption. Henry VI was mentally too feeble to rule unaided: a fact that was embarrassingly obvious when he had to be led by the hand as he paraded through London. Nevertheless, the chronicler Warkworth commented that Henry VI had never lost the love of his people, whereas Edward IV certainly had - his reign having occasioned 'much trouble and great loss of goods among the common people'.

Even allowing for Warkworth's pro-Lancastrian bias, it is possible that he is right in his view of the general unpopularity of Edward IV's government. This would explain Edward's failure to attract support both following the Warwick rebellion and when, in March 1471, he landed in Holderness to attempt to regain the kingdom. He found himself unable to gain access to the city of York without pretending that he had returned merely to claim his right to his dukedom.

However, as he marched south, Edward's support increased. In particular, Clarence returned to the fold. There could be little love lost between Lancastrians and Clarence at the best of times. He might have been dissatisfied with his position as brother to a king: but it was difficult to see how he could be more satisfied with his position under Henry VI, where he was the brother of that king's greatest enemy.

Edward IV regained his throne through battle. His rather casual approach to military campaigns was a thing of the past. He showed to the full a decisiveness and willingness to take risks that were rewarded by crushing victories. As always, there was the element of luck. Mist on the field and confusion in the Lancastrian ranks at Barnet played their part: the Neville brothers Warwick and Montagu lost their lives on the field of battle. At Tewkesbury, the king's forces emerged victorious from a conflict which left the Lancastrian line virtually non-existent. Prince Edward died on the field: Queen Margaret was captured shortly afterwards. Henry VI was murdered within days. In addition, the Beauforts lost Somerset and his brother, John Beaufort, and so were extinguished in the male line. Lancastrian claimants remained, of course, but the royal blood looked rather thin in the case of the most likely - or least unlikely - candidate, Henry, Earl of Richmond (see the genealogical table on page 2).

7 1471-83: The Calm before the Storm

A discussion of Edward IV's policies both foreign and domestic can be found on pages 120-41. Unsurprisingly, the death of so many opponents on and around the battlefield contributed greatly to the stability of the rest of Edward's reign. To be uncharitable, so did the death of the Duke of Clarence in February 1478. It was not surprising that Edward IV should have brought an act of attainder against his brother and secured his conviction on a charge of high treason. What is surprising is that it took the king so long to destroy him. It says much for Edward's patience that he tolerated his dangerous and wayward brother after treason, quarrel and provocation after provocation (see page 141).

There is little doubt that the England of 1471-83 was, by the standards of the previous 30 or so years, a stable country. Edward's subjects, as far as we can tell, seem to have thought so. Early Tudor writers, such as Polydore Vergil or Thomas More, used evidence from those who had lived through Edward's reign to produce their generally positive pictures of an effective monarch who had curbed civil war. Why, then, did it all fall apart in 1483? Why did Edward's early death on 9 April 1483 signal the collapse of his achievements and the destruction of his sons? Seeking an answer to these questions will involve a close examination of the circumstances around the actual usurpation.

8 Richard of Gloucester and the Attack on the Woodvilles

On the death of her husband, Queen Elizabeth attempted to claim a regency for herself. Her likely motive for this may well have been a deep distrust of the probable Protector, Richard of Gloucester. The council refused to accept her demands, and moved to appoint Gloucester as Protector until the young Edward V (aged 12) could be crowned - itself no more than a matter of months away. In all probability, Gloucester would then head the council for about four years until the king could take full control of government. However, Gloucester's distrust of the Woodvilles was at least the equal of their distrust of him. Accompanied by Henry Stafford, Duke of Buckingham, he intercepted the Woodville contingent taking Edward from Ludlow to London. Gloucester and Buckingham entertained Earl Rivers (formerly Sir Anthony Woodville) to dinner in Northampton on 29 April. The Gloucester charm did not last long. He arrested Rivers the next day. Richard immediately took control of Edward at Stony Stratford, arresting Richard Grey (the young king's half-brother) and Thomas Vaughan (Edward's Treasurer) for good measure. Rivers, Grey and Vaughan were despatched to Pontefract castle for later execution.

Why had all this happened? There are a number of possible explanations. The first is that Edward IV had created a situation in which major factional conflict simmered under the surface of an outwardly stable society, only to erupt once the king's restraining hand was gone. There is certainly strong evidence to support this interpretation. As we shall see in Chapter 5, Edward chose to rely heavily on a small number of great magnates to implement his policies and to maintain good order. The policy of relying on the Nevilles in the north collapsed with the Warwick rebellions, but Edward's overall method changed little following their eclipse. Where possible, he used members of the royal family. One of the greatest beneficiaries of Edward's patronage was his ever-loyal younger brother, Richard of Gloucester. Gloucester was able to build up a massive power-base in the north. In Wales and the Marches, power effectively rested with the Woodvilles - particularly Anthony, Earl Rivers. The north Midlands were dominated by Lord Hastings; Lancashire, Cheshire and parts of north-east Wales by the Stanleys. Unsurprisingly, the queen was eager for her husband to provide for her sons by her first marriage: Thomas Grey (Marquis of Dorset) and Richard Grey. We recall that the patronage offered was largely the result of dubious manipulation of the marriage market and the laws of inheritance. A good example is that of the Holland (dukes of Exeter) inheritance in the west country. The infant Anne (daughter of the Duchess of Exeter) was declared by Act of Parliament to be heiress to all the Exeter estates and was contracted in marriage to Dorset's son.

What was the effect of this policy of relying on these great magnates? First, there was the potential danger caused by the likely resentment of those magnates who felt left out from the inner circle. There are two obvious examples: Henry Stafford, Duke of Buckingham, and Ralph, Lord Neville (of the Holland family). Buckingham was squeezed out of the traditional rôle of the Staffords as great Marcher lords by the new Woodville power base, and at the same time, (see page 76), became a victim of the Woodville marriage market: he was 'provided' with a suitable wife - Katherine, a sister of the queen. As for Ralph, Lord Neville, (heir of the Earl of Westmorland), he was the principal loser in the Woodville manoeuvres over the Holland inheritance. So, both Buckingham and Lord Neville had little reason to love the Woodvilles or the king himself. Of course, in the short term that would matter little unless the king were weak. Edward IV was not. He had the appearance, vigour and bearing of a king. As we shall see in Chapter 6, once Edward had a firm hold on the kingdom his will was not to be trifled with. This does not mean, of course, that he was out to impose some new restraints on the nobility or that he sought to curb its power. He was more than happy to make full use of the nobility in its traditional rôle in preserving justice and good order. But it was clear that he would not tolerate dissent or unruliness. He won, therefore, obedience from his nobles. But from men like Buckingham and Lord Neville, this was only a grudging obedience.

However, obedience is one thing and loyalty to a dynasty is quite another. The problem is that Edward, in creating this inner ring of magnates, was leaving those at the periphery with less reason to feel loyalty to his children. This situation was compounded by the fact that his son and heir Edward was brought up entirely within the Woodville orbit: Earl Rivers was governor of Prince Edward's household at Ludlow. In fact, some might say, the prince was more of a Woodville than a York. This was no real problem, perhaps, while the father was there to groom and protect his children until they were adult and able to exercise power in their own right. But if he were not - then nobles like Buckingham and Neville had every reason to explore other possibilities. It is very significant that the pair chose to support the future Richard III.

To encourage the power of great magnates is not of itself dangerous to a king's authority. As was suggested in Chapter 2, a strong nobility could buttress a king's authority as long as the king maintained control of it. It is quite wrong to blame Edward IV for enabling Richard of Gloucester to build up a massive affinity on the grounds that this led to the usurpation. As Rosemary Horrox has argued, Gloucester's acquisition of his position 'would have been impossible without royal backing and reflected, rather than negated, royal authority'. However, it could be argued that rivalry *within* the magnate inner circle was a contributory factor to the downfall of Edward's dynasty - an indirect, short-term cause. But, of course, factional rivalry was present at the court of every medieval and early modern English monarch. What mattered was how well the monarch controlled it, and how deep and bitter the rivalry was. In Edward IV's case, he controlled the rivalry well: but it was nonetheless dangerously deep and bitter. Here we see again the main problem: the unpopularity of the Woodvilles, their awareness of that unpopularity and their understanding that their long-term safety rested on their relationship with the royal princes. Their most important adversaries were Hastings and Gloucester. Gloucester they resented because of his power in the north and the closeness of his relationship to the king. Hastings they resented not only because of his power, but also because of his personal friendship with and influence over Edward: allegedly, he encouraged Edward's interest in fleshly pleasures. It is characteristic of Edward IV that he should be well aware of the rivalries, but rely upon his personal authority and charisma to keep them under control. Not so easy, of course, after one is dead. It is very significant that, on his deathbed, Edward should demand a formal reconciliation between Hastings and Dorset: significant also that, as one commentator remarked, there remained a 'latent jealousy' despite the fair words. The episode, in fact, bears an uncomfortable resemblance to the equally futile 'love-day' between Margaret of Anjou and Richard of York. It is the refuge of a king whose policies have failed. And so it has to be said that Edward left a potentially destabilising legacy of distrust and hatred among his great magnates. What the late king's policies and over-confidence had bequeathed was the likelihood of a struggle for power over his sons. With that power, it was certainly possible that one or other faction would seek to destroy the other.

It is in this context that one must understand the attempts by the Woodvilles to prevent Gloucester from assuming the rôle of Protector, and of Gloucester and his supporters to prevent Elizabeth becoming regent. The writer of the Crowland Chronicle makes it clear that influential members of the council which met at Westminster after Edward's funeral were fearful of the consequences of a Woodville ascendancy.

1 The more farsighted members of the Council thought that the uncles and brothers [of the uncrowned Edward V] on the mother's side should be absolutely forbidden to have control of the person of the young man until he came of age ... [Lord Hastings] was afraid
5 that if supreme power fell into the hands of the queen's relatives they would then sharply avenge the alleged injuries done to them by that lord. Much ill-will, indeed, had long existed between Lord Hastings and them. However, the benevolent queen, wishing to extinguish every spark of murmuring and unrest, wrote to her son
10 that he should not have more than 2000 men when he came to London. This number was also pleasing to [Hastings], for he was confident enough, so it seemed, that the Dukes of Gloucester and Buckingham, in whom he had the greatest trust, would bring with them no less a number.

This is important because it provides evidence of the dangerous level of suspicion in the council and of the animosity between Hastings and the Woodvilles. How reliable is the chronicler? Inconveniently, we do not know the author. However, internal evidence suggests that he was a cleric and an administrator at the royal court, who attended council meetings, and that he wrote his political memoir in the spring of 1486. In other words, the author had every reason to know what he was talking about. There is also corroborative evidence from the contemporary Italian observer Dominic Mancini, who wrote:

1 [The] problem of the government during the royal minority was referred to the consideration of the barons. Two opinions were propounded. One was that the Duke of Gloucester should govern, because Edward in his will had so directed ... But this was the
5 losing resolution; the winning was that the government should be carried on by many persons among whom the duke .. should be accounted the chief ... All who favoured the queen's family voted for this proposal, as they were afraid that, if Richard took upon him

the crown or even governed alone, they, who bore the blame for
10 Clarence's death, would suffer death or at least be ejected from
their high estate.

According to common report, the chamberlain Hastings reported
all these deliberations by letter and messengers to the Duke of
Gloucester, because he had a friendship of long standing with the
15 Duke, and was hostile to the entire kin of the queen ... Besides, it
was reported that he had advised the duke to hasten to the capital
with a strong force, and avenge the insult done him by his enemies.
He might easily obtain his revenge if, before reaching the city, he
took the young King Edward under his protection and authority.

So far, then, it would seem that Edward's creation of a bitterly divided
inner circle made some sort of conflict very likely at his death. A.J.
Pollard (see Further Reading) is, however, keen to point out that there
was nothing inevitable in the conflict and suggested that evidence for
jealousies between the factions is limited. But, as we have seen,
contemporary commentators were very aware of the tensions between
the magnates, which focussed on a desire to control Edward V. Pollard
perhaps underestimates the depth of factional rivalry. In any case, even if
one accepts that there is only limited evidence for the tension, might this
not simply reflect Edward IV's undeniable ability to restrain it? And, if
the rivalry were not significant, then why did Hastings, Buckingham and
Gloucester move so swiftly against the Woodvilles?

It is one thing to argue, as is being done here, that Edward IV had left
a dangerous legacy of factional rivalry, but it is quite another to claim
that this rivalry led inevitably to the usurpation of the throne. It did not.
It led directly to the attack on the Woodvilles when Gloucester
intercepted the young Edward V on his way to London. This pleased
men such as Hastings, who were more than happy to see Woodville
presumption deflated. But this does not mean that they wanted
Gloucester to seize the throne. Hastings' loyalty to Edward IV and to his
sons was unquestioned. It was, in all probability, this loyalty that led to
his downfall at the hands of Gloucester (see page 86).

9 The Usurpation, 1483

Small wonder that the motives of Richard of Gloucester have fascinated
writers and historians up to the present day. On the one level, we have
the macabre, nephew-murdering villain of Sir Thomas More's *History of
King Richard III*, in which the king is, perhaps, used by More to warn of
the dangers of tyranny. Similarly, we have the evil hunchback of
Shakespeare's play, through whom phrases like 'the winter of our
discontent' have entered the language of modern political commentators. On the other hand, Richard has a society devoted to clearing his
name - the *Richard III Society* - whose activities range from amateur but

enjoyable works in his defence like Jeremy Potter's *Good King Richard?* to the commissioning and publishing of serious academic research into the period.

One of the main reasons for continued controversy over Gloucester's motives (and the actions of his reign) lies in the problematic nature of the contemporary or near-contemporary sources. Speculation on motives is difficult to accept from a source at the best of times, but there is little doubt that some sources attribute the worst motives to Richard for reasons of their own. Polydore Vergil's *Anglica Historia,* for example, has all the strengths of the best historical scholarship of its time and all the defects of a scholar who was encouraged to write the work by Richard's eventual nemesis, Henry VII. The work was dedicated to Henry VIII, and was therefore unlikely to be scrupulous in achieving a balanced picture. In particular, Vergil has the tendency to see deceit in Gloucester's every good action and to assume that Edward IV's death immediately aroused in Richard the ambition to become king. To a lesser extent, this tendency to use hindsight (the knowledge of what happened afterwards) to cover gaps in one's own knowledge afflicts the apparently neutral source written by Dominic Mancini, who developed a similarly unfavourable view of Gloucester's motives and what he saw as his 'insane lust for power'.

The problems with the sources are seized on by defenders of Richard III. The defenders' interpretations must be considered carefully, since they offer alternative explanations of the causes of the usurpation. The first issue concerns the execution of Lord Hastings on the orders of Gloucester on 13 June 1483. On the face of it, the ruthless destruction of his ally would seem to suggest that Richard was engaging in a preemptive strike. He knew that Hastings would never support his intended usurpation, and therefore removed him. Defenders, however, argue that Hastings was involved in a Woodville plot against the Protector, and that Gloucester was panicked into a swift counter-measure to defend his position. The problem with this relatively favourable view is that it is based on very little evidence. The only supporting evidence is a letter from Richard written to the city of York on the 10 June in which he appeals for help against a Woodville plot, but this is hardly an objective account of the situation. Horrox concludes that the Woodvilles were in disarray and no threat to the Protector in any case. Mancini says that Gloucester had used Buckingham to sound out the loyalty of Hastings and others: one can only speculate that Hastings had been revealed as an opponent to the deposition of Edward V. Our tentative conclusion must be that Hastings was executed because he was an obstacle to the ambitions of Richard.

Defenders also argue that Richard's own justification for taking the throne should not be dismissed. On 22 June, a certain Dr Ralph Shaw preached a remarkable sermon from St Paul's Cross, the official government pulpit in London. He seems to have alleged that Edward

IV's children were illegitimate, since the late king was bound by a form of marriage - technically, a pre-contract - to another woman before his marriage with Elizabeth Woodville. Charles Ross rightly concludes that there was absolutely no truth in these very convenient allegations. Richard himself implicitly confirmed their lack of truth when he showed interest in marrying Edward's eldest daughter, Elizabeth, after the death of his wife in March 1485. Would he have wanted to marry a bastard? There is also the account of the nearest contemporary chronicler, Mancini, who reports that Shaw alleged that Edward himself was illegitimate. If this is the case, then one can only be astonished at the fact that he had the audacity to accuse his own mother of adultery - a mother who was still living to hear the allegations, and whose piety was well known and recognised. In any case, if Richard truly took his stand on the laws of inheritance, then the young son of his elder brother, Clarence, had a better claim than him to the throne. The attainder against Clarence need not have prevented his son, Edward, Earl of Warwick, from becoming king. As it turned out, the unfortunate Warwick spent most of his life in the Tower of London.

So much for the arguments attributing Richard's usurpation to fear of Woodville-Hastings plots and his own conviction of the legality of the case. What we seem to be left with is his naked ambition. If ruthlessness is a sign of that ambition, then we need look no further than the illegal executions of Rivers, Grey and Hastings.

So, to summarise our analysis of the causes of the usurpation, we might argue as follows. One clear short-term cause was Edward IV's creation of an inner circle of magnates, which led to the dissatisfaction of those excluded from it. Some, like Buckingham, had little reason to be loyal to Edward IV's heirs. This cannot, of course, be seen in any way as a direct cause, although Buckingham was more than willing to support Gloucester's usurpation when the time came. A linked short-term cause was the serious tension between the Woodvilles, Gloucester and Hastings within that inner circle. Edward IV could and did control these tensions, but he could not control his early death. That death triggered a crisis in which those tensions surfaced in a struggle for the control of Edward V. This struggle need not have led to a usurpation, and therefore the issue of unresolved tensions within the inner circle can be seen as an important but indirect cause. The most important direct - and immediate - cause must be seen as the ambition and ruthlessness of Richard of Gloucester. One cannot blame Edward IV for not recognising this. Had Edward not died at 42, had he been able to pass on his throne to an adult son, then Richard of Gloucester probably would have been the epitome of the loyal brother and uncle of kings.

It is, however, possible to argue that Edward IV's decision to give his sons a Woodville upbringing was a serious mistake, given the hatred which other magnates felt towards the queen's family. Richard may have felt that his attack on the Woodvilles would simply rebound on him once one of their number took the throne. It is quite clear that the young Edward V objected vigorously when his uncle and Buckingham informed him of the arrest of the Woodvilles at Stony Stratford. Edward might be expected to take full control of his kingdom in, say, 1487 or 1488. All Richard could expect from him would be a swift revenge. So, to destroy the Woodville threat to himself, he had to seize the crown. If this argument is accepted, then it would make Edward's failure to allow for the bitter distrust of the Woodvilles a direct cause of the usurpation. On balance, this would be an overstatement. After all, Hastings was in a similar position to that of Gloucester. He disliked the Woodvilles and was prepared to assist with the removal of Edward V from their control. But there is no indication whatsoever that he thereafter felt the need to protect himself by encouraging the usurpation.

Perhaps the most satisfactory conclusion would be to argue that Richard of Gloucester's ambition was the most potent direct cause of the usurpation. That ambition was no doubt fuelled by his fear of the future consequences of his attack on the Woodvilles. It would, of course, take an unusual ruthlessness to act in the way he did. From what we know of Richard's character - particularly when we consider his treatment of Hastings - that ruthlessness was there in good measure.

10 The Reign of Richard III, 1483-5

A detailed analysis of Richard's government can be found in Chapter 6. What we are concerned with here is the causes of the two sets of conflicts in Richard's reign: the rebellion of 1483 (sometimes known as the Buckingham rebellion) and the invasion of Henry Tudor, Earl of Richmond, in 1485.

a) The Rebellion of 1483

This rebellion - or set of rebellions - broke out in the south and west of England in the autumn of 1483. Although the Duke of Buckingham became involved, it was in no sense 'his' rebellion. Nor can it be seen as a Lancastrian rising: many former Lancastrians had come to terms with Yorkist rule under Edward IV. The involvement of Henry Tudor seems to give the rebellion a Lancastrian colouring, but he may well have hoped simply for a restoration to his earldom under a released Edward V. However, rumours circulating that Richard had murdered the princes (the so-called 'Princes in the Tower') meant that he could, if necessary, be advanced as a candidate for the throne despite a weak claim. It is significant that he should stress his willingness to marry Elizabeth of York, Edward IV's eldest daughter, in order to appeal to Yorkist support. Indeed, this rebellion is best seen as a Yorkist one. It was not a rebellion dominated by those like the Woodvilles who had every reason to resent Richard. Instead, at its heart were men who had been closely identified with the government of Edward IV, and whom Richard III had deliberately retained in his service to emphasise continuity. That they should rise against him must be taken as indicative of their shock at his usurpation and their fear for the fate of Edward IV's sons. Of course, local rivalries, family ties and specific territorial ambitions doubtless also played their part. But it is clear that the unifying factor behind the rebellions was the dislike of what Richard of Gloucester had done.

Buckingham's motives are difficult to assess. He was, after all, closely identified with the usurpation, had acted as Richard's spokesman, and had received as much as he could reasonably hope by way of reward including the constableship of England. The Crowland chronicler says that John Morton, the Bishop of Ely, suggested that Buckingham should invite Henry Tudor to invade the country, to seize the crown and to marry Elizabeth of York. Polydore Vergil has a similar tale, although he states that Buckingham approached Morton with the plan. What we cannot know is why. It is possible that Buckingham joined in the rebellion because he thought it was going to succeed. After all, his experience under Richard had demonstrated the advantages of opportunism.

The rebellion scarcely even gathered momentum. Ironically, it was Buckingham's conspicuous failure to attract support in Wales that sapped the morale of the rebels. Henry Tudor's fleet sensibly turned tail: most of the leaders fled abroad. Nevertheless, the rebellion at least brought to the fore Richmond as a potential rival to Richard and therefore a focus for opposition to the king. It also exposed the partial failure of Richard III's policy of relying on Edward IV's former servants.

As we have suggested, the cause of the rebellion was Yorkist resentment at Richard's treatment of the sons of Edward IV rather than the ambition of the Duke of Buckingham. It is therefore not possible to argue that it was caused by an over-mighty noble. This is not to deny that Buckingham was such a noble. He was over-mighty because Richard had showered rewards on him following the extraordinary events of the usurpation. His decision to join in might be taken as a mark of his over-mighty status, which he was perhaps determined to preserve at all costs.

b) The Downfall of Richard III

The 1483 rebellion might have failed, but Richard had every reason to feel insecure. It was clear that he could not rely on the support of the nobles who were identified with the government of Edward IV. He increasingly relied upon those whose loyalty was to him rather than to the House of York as such. These were generally men who were part of his ducal affinity, built up in his brother's reign when he controlled the north in Edward's name. This meant that he felt the need to plant those northerners in key positions in the south. But he also recognised that his power-base was dangerously narrow as a result. It was, indeed, likely to increase resentment among the nobility of the south. It also meant that his northern supporters had a vested interest in discouraging Richard from attempting to widen that power-base. It was, for example, strongly rumoured that Richard wished to marry Elizabeth of York - in part to thwart Henry Tudor and in part to attempt to build bridges with the Woodvilles. But it seems that he was prevented from so doing by the threats of his northern supporters, who feared the consequences of a revival of Woodville power. The death of his only legitimate son, Edward, in April 1484 was a terrible blow. The future of his dynasty, if not his immediate hold on the throne, was called into question.

Richard III's problems did not lead directly to his defeat and death at Bosworth field. On 22 August 1485, he faced the army of the Earl of Richmond with a considerably larger force, but its effectiveness was compromised by rumours of treason: a reflection, perhaps, of the king's insecurity. Henry Tudor had landed on 7 August at Milford Haven and had made slow progress through Wales in the hope of attracting support. By the time he was facing the king's army, he had an inferior force and would need to rely on great good luck and/or desertions from Richard's side on the field of battle to stand a realistic chance of success. Henry had hoped that Thomas, Lord Stanley, who was his mother's second husband, would have declared for him. But the Stanleys were well known for their unwillingness to commit themselves until they had identified the winning side. The presence and aloofness of Lord Stanley and his brother, Sir William, on the battlefield worried both king and pretender. It is possible that the Earl of Northumberland, who was expected to fight for the king, similarly remained aloof from the battle. The contemporary evidence does not allow us to come to any firm conclusion, but we can be reasonably sure that Richard's death came about as a result of his decision to seek a swift end to the battle by leading a charge, accompanied by only his own household men, directly against Henry Tudor and his bodyguard. At this point, Sir William Stanley finally committed his forces to the battle. The king was surrounded and cut down.

Our conclusion must be that the battle was lost by the king rather than won by Henry Tudor. There was some treachery against Richard on the battlefield. But neither treason, possible lack of commitment among some of his followers, nor the king's narrow power-base led directly to defeat. The most immediate, direct and important cause of Richard's downfall was his own impulsive military gamble. Of course, it may be that the king's consciousness of the uncertain nature of his support propelled him into the fatal attempt to settle the business once and for all. But that we cannot know.

11 Henry VII and the End of the Wars of the Roses

It would be convenient for historians - and it certainly would have been for Henry VII - if the Wars of the Roses had ended as Richard's naked body was thrown over a horse and taken from Bosworth field. But the new king was likely to face challenges from the surviving members of the House of York and their adherents. The ten-year-old Earl of Warwick (son of the Duke of Clarence) was secure in the Tower, but this did not stop Yorkists from finding a look-alike imposter - one Lambert Simnel - to crown as Edward VI in the Yorkist stronghold of Dublin. Worryingly, Simnel was being used by Richard III's nephew, the Earl of Lincoln and Edward IV's sister, Margaret of Burgundy, as the focus for an invasion of England, backed by 2,000 German mercenaries. Henry VII defeated the rebel force in battle at Stoke (near Newark in Nottinghamshire) on 16 June 1487. Victory was not won easily. Nevertheless, Lincoln was killed on the field, and the imposter taken alive. He was humanely treated, and eventually gained safer employment as the king's falconer. This was not the end of the Yorkist threat. Henry VII was obliged to treat Yorkist plots seriously because they could be used by his fellow European princes as weapons to destabilise England. He also knew from his own experience how the chance of battle might turn against him. The battle of Stoke could easily have been Henry VII's Bosworth field.

In 1491, a further imposter emerged. From that date, a Flemish youth named Perkin Warbeck masqueraded as Richard of York (younger brother of Edward V and therefore one of the Princes in the Tower) in and out of the courts of Europe. The Holy Roman Emperor, Maximilian, recognised him as Richard IV. James IV of Scotland used him as the figure-head for an unsuccessful invasion of England in 1496. By 1497, however, Warbeck had run out of patrons and failed invasions, and surrendered to Henry. However, he could not resist further plotting and managed to get both himself and the hapless Earl of Warwick executed in 1499.

Even then, Yorkist plots did not cease. The remaining close relations of Edward IV, the de la Pole family, continued to intrigue against the king from their places of exile. So, when was the last blow of the Wars of the Roses finally struck? It is possible to make a case for Warbeck's last military action at Exeter in 1497, but the full-scale battle at Stoke is usually seen as the end of it all.

Clearly, the Simnel rebellion was dynastic in origin. To a lesser extent the same is true of Warbeck, although the dynastic question was more obviously exploited by Henry's fellow monarchs. Henry VII's dynasty survived the Yorkist challenge in part because he maintained a most effective surveillance system and in part because he largely succeeded in controlling his nobility through a system known as recognisances (see page 11). Also, despite the Yorkist plots, Henry secured the service of former adherents of the Yorkist kings at court and in his administration.

Even those who fought against him at Bosworth field were offered the opportunity to prove their loyalty to the new régime. Perhaps the most important factor in his success was that he was able to do what Edward IV and Richard III had failed to do: survive long enough for a son to succeed him without a minority.

12 The Theme of the Over-mighty Noble: A Summing Up

Examiners - quite rightly - like candidates who are prepared to explore themes (sets of linked ideas or information) rather than those who simply provide a grind through material in date order. Themes are useful in that they can, where appropriate, reveal underlying causes which can be obscured by a purely chronological discussion. We have discussed in passing the argument that an over-mighty nobility caused the Wars, and felt that this was by no means appropriate in every conflict. But we should, perhaps, review the issue to make sure that we have not lost sight of the overall picture.

So - to what extent is it true that an over-mighty nobility was responsible for the Wars? Our first problem is one of definition. What is an over-mighty noble? Perhaps we can take the phrase to refer to a noble whose power and ambition were directed at the overthrow of the power of the monarch. This might or might not involve an actual usurpation. How useful is this definition when applied to the obvious candidates?

As far as Richard of York is concerned, the concept is of limited value at best. We suggested earlier that his rebellion was caused, not because he was an over-mighty noble, but because his position was threatened through the failures of the king and the aggression of Margaret of Anjou. His son, Edward, clearly fits the definition in the sense that he openly and deliberately sought to destroy Henry VI. But it must not be forgotten that the stimulus behind his assault on the throne was not so much his status as an over-mighty noble as the fact that he inherited his father's cause.

The Earl of Warwick, however, is a very strong candidate indeed. We have seen that he sought to maintain an unrealistic dominance over the king and was prepared to use rebellion and treason to uphold it. His attitude was the product of the special circumstances of the usurpation - which gave him that power in the first place - and his own gross ambition. He cannot therefore be seen as typical of an over-mighty class which supposedly dominated the period of the Wars. A number of over-mighty nobles developing out of special circumstances does not make an over-mighty nobility as a whole. In any case, Edward IV was able to impose his authority over the nobility after Warwick's defeat. Had the country been teeming with over-mighty nobles, then this would have been a near-impossibility.

There was little evidence from his brother's reign that Richard of Gloucester was an over-mighty noble, since his power served and complemented that of the king. However, he became an over-mighty noble with a vengeance due to the sudden flowering of his ambition in the crisis after Edward IV's premature death.

The Duke of Buckingham fits our definition in exactly the same way as Warwick. He too acquired a dominant position following a usurpation, and it is likely enough that his rebellion against Richard III was stimulated by his belief that he could defend that position only through joining what he wrongly thought was the winning side.

And finally, does Henry Tudor fit the definition? He was certainly successful in overthrowing the power of a king, but it is difficult to see him as an over-mighty noble for the simple reason that he himself lacked personal power in England, from where he was a long-term exile.

It would seem, then, that the concept of the over-mighty nobility is of some value, but its importance can easily be over-estimated. We have rejected the idea that the nobility as a whole was over-mighty. We have suggested that powerful nobles became over-mighty ones only when a set of extraordinary circumstances arose that stimulated their unusually strong ambitions and ruthless greed. And so, we should accept that we can adopt the concept as a useful means of comparison and, therefore, of combining information. But it is not particularly helpful to see it as a fundamental cause of the conflicts.

13 Conclusion

The conflicts during the reigns of Henry VI, Edward IV, Richard III and Henry VII did not have identical causes. The outbreak of the Wars of the Roses under Henry VI reflected that king's failure to meet the genuine challenges of kingship. These failures resulted in the alienation of the Duke of York and his allies from the Lancastrian régime, which in turn led to a dynastic conflict when the king's insanity brought to prominence his queen and her desire to destroy the York family in order to protect her son. We argued that, although there were long-term tensions within late medieval society, an effective king might use them to buttress his power.

Edward IV, unlike Henry VI, was an effective king. The rebellions in his reign were fuelled by a struggle with the Lancastrians, but the most important cause was not dynastic rivalry but the willfulness, ambition and arrogance of the king-making Earl of Warwick. Warwick was an over-mighty noble indeed. His excessive power was the result of the great contribution he had made to Edward's usurpation. Edward IV could not afford to let him retain a completely unchallenged supremacy among the nobility. For his part, Warwick was simply incapable of recognising that no king could afford to grant the virtually vice-regal status he demanded. Edward duly worked to establish other power-blocs to reduce his reliance on Warwick, but he did not do so aggressively. Warwick was never excluded from the king's favour and patronage. But the earl chose to brood over his resentment rather than attempt to curb it by recognising that the king's actions made political sense. It was the Woodville marriage, with its major impact on the sensitive noble marriage market, that inflamed further that massive and increasingly resentful ego to the point of rebellion. There is little difference in the two Warwick rebellions, save that he played the dynastic card in his second rebellion in the absence of alternatives.

The usurpation of Richard of Gloucester had different causes. It will not do to argue that the usurpation was simply the standard behaviour of the familiar 'over-mighty noble'. In the context of Edward IV's reign, it is difficult to attach that label to Richard of Gloucester. He was very powerful (particularly in the north of the country), but that power was used in the service of the king. That Gloucester chose to use his power to overthrow his nephew is a direct result of the flowering of a ruthless ambition which Edward could not have anticipated. It is true that the early and unexpected death of Edward IV brought to the surface the dangerous tensions between the Woodvilles and other factions which had been controlled, but never resolved, by the king. It is true that Richard may have felt that, even if he moved against the Woodvilles, he would never be safe because Edward V would seek revenge in the Woodville name once his minority came to an end. But, in the end, such rationalisations cannot offer the full explanation: we are left with a ruthlessness and violence that shocked hardened contemporaries. The direct cause of the usurpation rests with the psyche of Richard III, and that we can never fully understand.

The conflicts in the reign of Richard III appear on the surface to be dynastic: the attempt to replace the dynasty of York with the vaguely Lancastrian dynasty of the Tudors. However, the first rebellions in 1483 were primarily a Yorkist protest against the usurpation, with the hope that the sons of Edward IV might be alive and rescuable. As that hope faded, Henry Tudor attracted support in the absence of other pretenders. His success at Bosworth owed as much to luck and to his opponent's tactical mistakes as it did to the unpopularity of Richard III. In turn, the conflicts in Henry VII's reign were caused not by the king's policies but by those members of the House of York who were unwilling to accept his dynasty as one offering a new unity.

Finally, we should, perhaps, beware of interpretations that place undue stress on the fundamental instability of late medieval English society. It was accepted in Chapter 2 that kings faced real challenges as they dealt with such issues as the great and increasingly powerful nobles and bastard feudalism. One could also argue that the violence of Henry VI's reign encouraged the ambitious and ruthless noble to believe that rebellion was a useful form of power politics. But such challenges could be met. For the last dozen or so years of his reign, Edward IV was able, by and large, to impose his will upon the nobility. Had he lived another few years, we might now be saying that the Wars of the Roses ended in

1471. If Richard III had emerged as the victor at Bosworth field, then it is perfectly possible that his régime could have stabilised as his power-base gradually widened. In any case, as we shall see in Chapter 6, Henry VII was able to control his nobility very effectively indeed.

Making notes on *'The Downfall of the Yorkist Kings and the End of the Wars of the Roses'*

As you make notes, bear in mind the aims of the chapter. Since we are primarily discussing the causes of the conflicts, your note-making must seek, not only to cover the arguments, but also to provide the necessary detail to back them up.

1   Introduction
1.1   What argument is the chapter going to adopt?
2.   The Reign of Edward IV, 1461-71: Problems facing the New King
2.1   The Long-term Problem of the Power of the Nobility. In what ways had the Wars left a difficult legacy for Edward IV?
2.2   An Immediate Problem: the Defeated Lancastrian Nobility. Why did the king seek to attract former Lancastrians? How sensible and successful was his policy?
2.3   The Problem of Warwick. Outline the king's policy towards Warwick.
3.   The Woodville Marriage. How unsuitable was the Woodville marriage? What was its short-term impact?
4.   Warwick in Rebellion, July-October 1469. Describe the course of the rebellion, and explain why Warwick was obliged to release the king. What were the causes of the Warwick rebellion?
5.   Warwick's Second Rebellion, March 1470. Briefly describe the course of the rebellion, Warwick and Clarence's exile and the flight of Edward IV.
6.   The Readeption and Edward IV's recovery of the throne. How was Edward IV able to recover his throne?
7.   The Calm before the Storm. Notes not needed.
8.   Richard of Gloucester and the attack on the Woodvilles.
8.1   What were Gloucester's initial steps against the Woodvilles?
8.2   Why did Buckingham and Lord Neville lack commitment to Edward's dynasty?
8.3   Did Edward IV's failure to resolve below-the-surface factional conflict lead directly to the usurpation?
9.   The Usurpation, 1483. How meaningful were the reasons given by Richard of Gloucester for taking the throne?
10.   The Reign of Richard III, 1483-5
10.1 What are the two sets of conflicts in Richard's reign?
10.2 The rebellion of 1483. Why did the rebellion break out? What were Buckingham's motives? What is the significance of the rebellion in

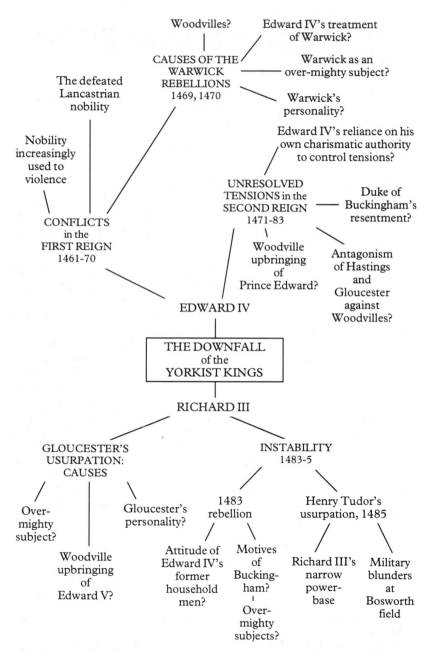

Summary - The Downfall of the Yorkist Kings and the End of the Wars of the Roses

terms of the Earl of Richmond?

10.3 The Downfall of Richard III. What problems did Richard face in the search for support? Why did Richard III lose the battle of Bosworth field?

11. Henry VII and the end of the Wars of the Roses

11.1 How much of a threat to Henry VII were Simnel and Warbeck?

11.2 What were the motives of those supporting the two pretenders?

11.3 Discuss the issue of when the Wars of the Roses finally came to an end.

12. The Theme of the Overmighty Subject: A Summing Up

13. Conclusion
Use Sections 12 and 13 to to help you plan essays. Notes not needed.

Answering essay questions on 'The Downfall of the Yorkist Kings and the End of the Wars of the Roses'

It is most unlikely that examiners would set an essay question which did not demand a discussion of the outbreak of the Wars of the Roses. And so, this chapter, together with Chapter 3, has equipped you to handle the more wide-ranging question covering all or most of the various conflicts of the Wars.

From what you have read in Chapters 3 and 4, it should be clear that you should not accept the argument that the conflicts had identical causes. In the *Answering essay questions* section to Chapter 3, you were given some ideas about how to structure your essay around a statement of argument. It might be helpful at this stage to consider the issue of the essay plan, which is particularly vital when essays are wide-ranging. I would argue that a good plan helps you to get your argument clear in your mind. The plan is where you jot down the main headings which may well form the longer paragraphs of your essay. Perhaps an example would be helpful at this point. Suppose you are faced with a typical question: 'The Wars of the Roses, c.1459 to 1485 were mainly caused by the personal failings of kings'. Comment on this view.' Your plan would enable you to identify the following conflicts:

Outbreak: Richard of York 1461	1469-71: Warwick Rebellions/Readeption/ Edward IV recovers throne	Gloucester Usurpation/ 1483 rebellion/ 1485 Henry Tudor

Using these headings, you might try to list the appropriate causes in one or two words.

What you should now have is the outline of your argument. You may feel that there is some truth in the statement in the question, but hopefully you have seen that it is more appropriate for the first set of causes than it is for the others. And it ignores the longer-term problems in society which were not caused by the weaker kings as such but were certainly made worse by them.

Here are some more essay titles. Write plans for each, followed by your opening paragraph and using the format suggested in the Chapter 3 guidance section.

1   How far were the Wars of the Roses (up to 1487) caused by the ambitions of greedy nobles?
2   'The phrase "Wars of the Roses" is a misnomer, since the conflicts between c.1455 and 1487 had little in common.' How far do you accept this view?
3   To what extent was a fundamental instability in society primarily to blame for the Wars of the Roses (up to 1497)?

A word of warning on plans. It is very tempting to overdo them. Examiners frequently complain about over-elaborate plans which must have taken 15 minutes to write - and that is at least 10 minutes of essay-writing time wasted. Writing plans quickly and efficiently needs practice.

Source-based questions on *'The Downfall of the Yorkist Kings and the End of the Wars of the Roses'*

1. Conflict in the council after the death of Edward IV.
Read the extracts from the Crowland Chronicle and Dominic Mancini on pages 84-5. Answer the following questions:
a)   From internal evidence alone, how objective are the two sources? (3 marks).
b)   What are the similarities and differences between the two accounts of deliberations within the council? (6 marks).
c)   What more would you need to know about the Crowland Chronicler and the Italian Dominic Mancini before you could make a judgment of their respective reliability and accuracy? (6 marks).

CHAPTER 5

The Impact of the Wars of the Roses

1 Introduction

In 1930, W.C. Sellar and R.J. Yeatman wrote their wonderfully original and comic *1066 And All That*. In the 'Compulsory Preface (This means You)' the authors said:

> 1 History is not what you thought. It is what you can remember. All
>   other history defeats itself. This is the only Memorable History of
>   England, because all the History that you can remember is in this
>   book, which is the result of years of research in golf-clubs,
> 5 gun-rooms, green-rooms, etc.

Quite. And this is what their extensive research has to tell us about the Wars of the Roses:

> 1 Noticing suddenly that the Middle Ages were coming to an end,
>   the Barons now made a stupendous effort to revive the old Feudal
>   amenities of Sackage, Carnage, and Wreckage and so stave off the
>   Tudors for a time. They achieved this by a very clever plan, known
> 5 as the Wars of the Roses (because the barons all picked different
>   coloured roses in order to see which side they were on).

The authors then list a set of questions to be demanded of any baron aspiring to be king. These include:

> Are you insane? If so, state whether permanently or only
> temporarily.

The book only works, of course, if the reader knows enough to spot the deliberate exaggerations, errors, half-truths and apparent misunder-standings. In this case, the reader is expected to know that the Wars of the Roses were a time of great turmoil, violence, conflict and destruction: and, perhaps, that the reference to the 'different coloured roses' is a suitably garbled version of a scene in Shakespeare's *Henry VI, Part 1* Shakespeare shows a quarrel between Richard of York and the Earl of Somerset, in which York demands:

> Let him that is a true-born gentleman,
> And stands upon the honour of his birth,
> If he suppose that I have pleaded truth,
> From off this brier pluck a white rose with me.

Somerset responds:

> Let him that is no coward nor no flatterer,
> But dare maintain the party of the truth,
> Pluck a red rose from off this thorn with me.

The scene concludes with threats of violence. York says 'I dare say that this quarrel will drink blood another day'. The members of Shakespeare's audience could nod heads sagely, knowing that the Wars of the Roses were conflicts of unprecedented savagery. Or at least, they thought they knew. Sixteenth-century writers had, after all, been adamant that the Wars *were* devastating. They claimed that noble families were simply wiped out on blood-soaked battlegrounds, that brother killed brother, and that father killed son in a hellish anarchy worse than any campaign of the Hundred Years War.

Here, then, is the common interpretation which lies behind the late sixteenth-century drama of Shakespeare and the early twentieth-century humour of Sellar and Yeatman. But we need not accept it as fact. As we shall see, there are plenty of modern historians who would wish to dismiss it as the product of distortion and propaganda. It is therefore the task of this chapter to assess the impact of the Wars of the Roses, both short and long term, on England.

But what is meant by 'impact'? If we simply looked at, say, the effect of the wars on the nobility, then this would be unjustifiably narrow. If we looked at impact on 'England', then this would be unjustifiably imprecise. Perhaps the best step would be to handle the issue of impact on England by seeking the answers to a number of broad questions, using a method of dividing up large issues which is familiar to historians: in other words, to assess the political, social and economic impact of the Wars.

2 The Political Impact of the Wars of the Roses

Politics is (arguably) more than 'government'. In a wider sense, politics is concerned with power relationships of every type (hence phrases like 'office politics'). Within the context of the Wars of the Roses, we need to discuss such issues as the effect of the Wars on kingship and on the different social classes of England.

a) Did the Wars of the Roses damage the theory of kingship?

It seems hardly likely that the Wars of the Roses could enhance kingship. Indeed, it might be thought that the deposition - and death in violent circumstances - of kings might have endangered the very institution of monarchy. It might have led to nobles questioning the value of kingship itself. However, it can be stated quite bluntly that this never happened.

Not even in the realms of idle theorising was such a step contemplated. And why not? The answer is simple enough. Kingship was fundamental to the power structure of feudal England. To take away the monarchy meant the breaking of that chain of land ownership on which power was based. By what right did a noble retain land, if a king's right were taken away? Why should the nobility exist, if the king did not? As for government by, say, a council of nobles, this was never seen as anything other than an unfortunate necessity. The joy that greeted the recovery of Henry VI from his first bout of madness is a clear testimony to this.

b) Did the wars damage royal authority and increase the power of the nobility in the long term?

Even if the monarchy were unchallenged in theory, it might be expected that its powers would be irreparably damaged by the wars. At the very least, Henry VI's incompetence would do little for the prestige of kingship. Mayhem, rebellion and the deposition of kings were all factors likely to encourage the unruly and over-mighty noble to expand his power at the king's expense. And, of course, that noble could exploit the possibility of rival claims to the throne to enhance that power. Warwick and Buckingham would seem to be the obvious examples. Of course, this argument was examined in Chapter 4 as we sought to establish whether or not the continuing conflict under Edward IV, Richard III and Henry VII reflected a real shift in power away from the king. The argument was rejected on the grounds that both Edward IV (in the last 12 years of his reign) and Henry VII were able to impose their personal authority on the nobility. It has to be said that there were significant differences in the way in which Edward and Henry treated the nobility. Edward was prepared to follow the traditional pattern of granting a trusted noble the right to govern a particular region in a near-autonomous manner. Henry VII started out in a similar way. His uncle and chief supporter Jasper Tudor, Duke of Bedford, was given control of Wales (where he had his own power-base). But, on Bedford's death, the king governed Wales through a council whose leader - the Bishop of Lincoln - had little personal power in the region.

Edward IV controlled his nobility through the force of his own authority as communicated by his impressive and suitably-charismatic personality. Henry VII might be profoundly uncharismatic, but he was certainly systematic. And he systematically tightened his control over the nobility by entrapping them in a web of recognisances (see page 11). There was nothing new in a king enforcing recognisances to secure good behaviour - Richard III in particular had made considerable use of them - but Henry adopted them on a scale that is an abundant testimony to his political understanding and cool-headed ruthlessness. Polydore Vergil commented:

1 The king wished (as he said) to keep all Englishmen obedient
  through fear ... All of his subjects who were men of substance when
  found guilty of whatever fault he harshly fined ... to make the
  population less well able to undertake any upheaval and to
5 discourage at the same time all offences.

There was a further element in Henry VII's increased ascendancy over
the nobility. Unlike Edward IV, he was anything but generous in his
patronage. Offices or land were not distributed to secure loyalty. No
magnate received anything simply because he was a magnate. Instead,
what grants were made had to be earned by service. And Henry made
sure that he kept as much of the land forfeited to the crown as possible.
For example, he retained the lands formerly held by Richard III in the
north. Since land meant power in both a local and national sense, the
crown gained in strength as a direct result of this policy. In fact, it could
be argued that the Wars of the Roses - or, at least, the conflict with
Richard III - actually increased the power of the king through giving him
the opportunity to accumulate more land throughout the country.

    And so, despite the crises of Richard III's reign, Henry VII was able to
secure a control over the nobility which was greater than that of Edward
IV. Clearly, then, the Wars of the Roses did not lead to a long-term gain
in power for the nobility at the expense of the monarch. Instead, one
might argue that the Wars of the Roses were useful to the Tudor dynasty
as propaganda to discourage those dissatisfied with the régime from
flirting with rebellion. This was done by making sure that the Wars were
presented as a murderous and bloody disaster for the whole kingdom.

c) What impact did the Wars of the Roses have on justice and law and order?

It makes sense to deal with law and order at this point, because, as was
suggested on page 36, the nobility played a vital part in royal justice and
the maintenance of peace. But it was also pointed out that the nobles
were themselves the likely subverters of justice and peace when it suited
their own interests to be so. Since it has been argued that the nobility did
not gain in power as a result of the Wars, logic would dictate that it
should also be argued that the nobility was unable to corrupt law and
order in the long term. Fortunately, this would seem to be the case.

    Of course, this is not to deny that it was symptomatic of the weakness
of royal authority under Henry VI that royal justice should be flouted
and that law and order in the regions should be at the mercy of those
connected with the dominant faction at court. But then, these problems
arose out of Henry VI's personality and pre-dated the outbreak of the
Wars themselves. Military conflict inevitably dislocated royal authority
even further. Nevertheless, Edward IV was able to restore that authority
to some degree. He re-established the supervisory rôle of the king over

the judicial system. He had the power and self-confidence to intervene personally in major breaches of the peace (see page 125). He also increased the power of justices of the peace to try criminal cases by transferring that power from the notoriously corrupt sheriffs, who were all too often the creatures of the local magnate.

But this does not mean that Edward sought to remove the influence of the great magnates over local law and order. As was argued above, the king was happy enough to rely on trusted nobles to control parts of the kingdom in his name, and he continued the traditional practice of appointing magnates to head the commissions of the peace for the English counties. In short, he expected his magnates to curb outrageous violence and civil disorder, but he most emphatically did not expect them to create oases of peace, tranquillity and an entirely objective and fair legal system in which they (the nobles) were treated in exactly the same manner as the poorest peasant. After all, law and order interested the king in so far as it affected his power and position. Major riots and blatant subversion of the legal system threatened his prestige and his authority, and so had to be curbed. Within limits, they were. No doubt the nobles were not averse to manipulating their continuing influence over the system, and no doubt many crimes and criminals went unpunished. But these, Edward did not see as a political threat. So, he was not prepared to invest the time and energy in a struggle which would have necessitated a change in his attitude to the nobility. If he had wished to put a complete stop to the disorder and violence of the aristocracy, he would have had to put a stop to the illegal retaining of followers. He had the backing in law to do so, and even took the step in 1468 of having an Act passed which made retaining itself illegal (except for household servants and legal agents). But this was no more than a warning shot across the bows to keep the aristocracy on the right course: as far as we know, the Act was never enforced. Edward IV did not lack fellow-feeling for the noble caste from which he had emerged. It was foreign to his outlook to wish to limit its traditional influence, or its sources of power. He needed powerful nobles, as his power exploited theirs.

So, the experience of the Wars of the Roses did not lead Edward IV into a major campaign against either the power of the nobility over law and order or the level of everyday violence in society. The gravest abuses of the worst days of Henry VI were no more, but there is no justification for arguing that the improvement was remarkable. There is little reliable statistical evidence that is relevant, and, although Parliament's frequent complaints about lawlessness and the many petitions it received alleging persistent disorder must be taken seriously, provided that allowances are made for likely exaggeration, there is no reason to blame the Wars of the Roses for this seemingly high level of violence, which was typical of late medieval England.

It seems likely that public order improved somewhat in the reign of

Henry VII. The king further increased the power of the justices of the peace in a move towards greater central control of law enforcement. But there is no doubt that Henry's effective control of the nobility played a greater part in maintaining public order than any such administrative reform.

Our conclusion should be that the impact of the Wars of the Roses on law and order was limited in the long term. In the short term (i.e. during the reign of Henry VI), there is little doubt that the Wars significantly worsened the already shaky judicial system as nobles used the opportunities created by civil war to pursue private feuds by violent means. However, it is clear that, in the longer term, Edward IV curbed the graver excesses of the nobility, but was not stimulated by his experience of the breakdown of law and order to attempt to tackle the major problem - the nobility itself and its excessive power over local justice. Henry VII was more effective in this area as a by-product of his politically-motivated desire to control his nobles through fear.

d) Did the Wars of the Roses weaken the position of the nobility?

We have already seen that, thanks to the successes of Edward IV and Henry VII, kingship emerged from the Wars of the Roses alive and well. So now, we should turn the question on its head. Was the position of the nobility under threat from a reinvigorated kingship? Chapter 6 investigates the usefulness of the concept of New Monarchy, whose adherents argue that, following the Wars of the Roses, kings were able to increase their own power at the expense of that of the nobility. Did, then, the Wars stimulate an awareness on the king's part that a powerful nobility had to be curbed once and for all? And did kings take steps to do so? Under Edward IV, the answers to both questions are certainly no. The existing position of the nobility was not under any sort of threat. Edward, as we have seen, was content to encourage the growth of great magnate power-blocs (Gloucester, the Woodvilles) and relied upon his own charismatic personality to control them. It is significant that Edward should increase the numbers of peers during his reign. Alexander Grant has calculated that the extinction and forfeiture rate under Edward IV was 25 per cent: where, in other words, the male line of the family died out, or the peer was deprived of his title through treason. But the replacement rate was 31 per cent. Significantly, the extinction rate under Henry VII was 42 per cent, but his replacement rate was a mere 17 per cent. The very top ranks of the peerage (earls, marquesses, and dukes) were increased from 7 to 12 under Edward: Henry started with 16, but, by the end of his reign, there were only 10. This reluctance to maintain numbers among the magnate class can, perhaps, be seen as part and parcel of the king's desire to subject the nobility to stricter controls. But there was not - and could not be - any suggestion of the king destroying the nobility. What he wanted to do was to make sure that the power was his to call upon, and that no noble became so dominant that the king needed to beg.

But does this mean that we can say that the Wars of the Roses actually stimulated Henry VII's ruthless treatment of the nobility? There is simply no way of telling for sure. Henry's youth was certainly scarred by 14 years of exile at the court of Brittany: an exile brought about by the changing fortunes of the Wars. In 1471, he became the main Lancastrian claimant to the throne following the murder of Henry VI and the death his son, Edward. Because of this, he was swept out of danger to Brittany by his uncle, Jasper Tudor. It is conceivable that the experience of insecurity led him to seek stability by clamping down on the nobility. If one accepts this view, then it is possible to suggest the most tentative of indirect links between the Wars of the Roses and the significant reduction in the power and autonomy of the nobility during Henry VII's reign.

3 The Social Impact of the Wars of the Roses

1 What misery, what murder and what execrable plagues this famous
  region hath suffered by the division and dissension of the
  renowned houses of Lancaster and York, my wit cannot
  comprehend nor my tongue declare, neither yet my pen fully set
5 forth.

So said the Tudor historian Hall, whose *The Union of the Two Noble and Illustre Families of Lancaster and York* was published in 1548. Hall describes a society in chaos. The implication is that the effect of the Wars was felt by all social classes. The impression given is that fear stalked town and village alike, that city dwellers cowered behind their reinforced walls, and that by the firesides of the aristocracy, grieving widows wept. We are invited to believe that intellectual and cultural life was swept away: a memory of light in the darkness. But is it true? Was English society devastated? Was ordinary life in ruins?

As we examine various aspects of English society in search of an answer, it is necessary to keep in mind a note of caution. Many of the sources on which we are forced to rely give only a very partial picture, and are frequently downright unreliable and untrustworthy. The conclusions we can grope towards are inevitably tentative.

a) The Duration of the Wars

It makes sense to argue that the longer the country was gripped by war, the more suffering resulted and the more everyday life was dislocated. The problem is that there is little agreement among historians as to how long the actual warfare lasted. For a start, there are definition problems.

What does 'actual warfare' mean? If we define it simply as the time spent on the field of battle, then this would quite wrongly ignore the disruptive military preparation, the long marches towards battle, the skirmishes and even those would-be combatants who simply did not arrive in time - or in the right place - to fight. We can certainly disregard as a gross underestimate the historian Lander's view that the total period of 'active campaigning' between 1455 and 1487 (the first battle of St Albans to the battle of Stoke) amounted to about 13 weeks. In the Appendix to his book *The Wars of the Roses: Military Activity and English Society, 1452-97*, Anthony Goodman considers slightly different dates (1455-85) but concludes that there were 'at least 61 weeks' domestic campaigning.' Perhaps the most convincing and judicious estimate is by A.J. Pollard, who takes into account fighting on the borders of the kingdom as well as the major set-piece battles: and he suggests over two years of campaigning between the same dates. Such figures, however, are not particularly revealing in themselves. It will be necessary to examine other issues before the actual effect of this amount of fighting can be gauged.

b) How many were involved in the military campaigns?

This issue is a nightmare for those who like precision. For those who like to sift and weigh, to tease the less uncertain out of a morass of uncertainty, then to attempt to establish the possible numbers of participants is a real (and enjoyable) challenge.

But why is this so problematic? The difficulty lies in the scarcity and gross distortions of the sources. In fact, we lack any firm statistical evidence. Most chroniclers were absent from the battle and wrote well after the events they described. Some were clerics, and so ignorant of military matters that, in any case, their presence would probably not have improved their accuracy. On the rare occasions when we do get an eyewitness account we are little better off. A London chronicle probably written by William Gregory suggested a huge figure of 100,000 Yorkists alone at the second battle of St Albans. At least he was present (in Warwick's army), although we cannot know how he estimated the number the soldiers. But any claim that might be made that he was reliable is totally destroyed by some frankly ludicrous figures he burdens us with for the battle of Towton. This was seen as the most bloody of the conflicts of the Wars of the Roses, but, even so, we cannot accept that virtually every adult male in England was fighting on the battlefield. And this is what his figures suggest. As Charles Ross has pointed out, with a total population of, say, two and a half million, England would have had about 600,000 men able to pick up a weapon. But Gregory's figures would have us believe that nearly 500,000 of those were hammering away at each other in fields near Tadcaster one snowy day in 1461.

Can we approach a more exact figure for the Wars as a whole by establishing the number of magnates involved? After all, the scale of a battle would depend on the number of magnates present. A magnate would call upon his gentry retainers (or at least those whose function was mainly a military one). These retainers would be under the obligation to provide a specified number of fighting men. If we could establish a sound estimate for the numbers of men brought by a typical magnate, then a meaningful approximate figure for participants might emerge. It is certainly worth a try.

Now, an examination of the few surviving contracts suggests that the retainer would be expected to provide perhaps five men. We also know that, in cases of need, the nobility would also call out their tenants to fight, although, of course, they were unlikely to be as well trained as the retainers. There were certainly more tenants than retainers and retainers' men. If we take an example from the *Paston Letters* and assume that it is representative, then we see John Howard, Duke of Norfolk, agreeing to provide a substantial force for Richard III. Just under two-thirds of the 800 men he gathered were tenants. So, we might do some straightforward calculations based on these figures to come up with what would appear at first sight to be that reasonably meaningful estimate for the numbers of men involved. Unfortunately, this will not work. Even apart from the various suppositions and guesswork, we simply do not know how many nobles were involved in many of the conflicts. Nor can we come up with a meaningful figure for the number of retainers involved. Any attempted generalisation (so many retainers per noble) is rendered near-useless by the fact that some magnates (particularly those in the troubled north) had a much greater number of trained fighting men available than did other magnates. Nor would all retainers be prepared to fight if, say, it would mean breaking their allegiance to the king.

So, what are we left with? Disagreement among historians, for a start. C.F. Richmond, for example, has argued that only 6 peers fought for Richard III at Bosworth field, but Charles Ross suggests around 20. Ross relies on a narrative poem known as *The Ballad of Bosworth Field*, which he feels was written by a northerner who was well informed on the nature of Richard's support. Perhaps so, but it has to be said that the poet praises Sir William Stanley (who fought against Richard at Bosworth) with some enthusiasm. It would be tempting for the poet to exaggerate Richard's strength to make Stanley's rôle in his defeat seem even more praiseworthy. The poem explicitly states that the king's army alone stood at '40,000 and 3': Ross himself thinks that between 8,000 and 10,000 was much more likely. A.J. Pollard discusses the figures outlined by Richmond and Ross in his usual balanced manner, but without coming to any firm conclusion (or figure) for participants. Nevertheless, he argues that the evidence at least suggests that peers did not hold themselves aloof from the conflict of the Wars of the Roses. Taking the period 1469-71, Pollard argues that 30 out of roughly 48 to

50 available peers were directly involved in military conflict. Others stayed clear of involvement, but must nevertheless have made substantial military preparations - if for no other reason than to defend the fence upon which they were sitting.

So, we have a very considerable involvement of peers in the conflicts. The impact of this is felt by retainers and tenants alike: and it must therefore seem clear that the impact on English society at village level was itself considerable. However, it should be made clear that the peasantry itself was virtually never called upon to fight. The reason is simple enough: the nobility had little or no desire to arm men whose interest in dynastic squabble was likely to be significantly less than their hatred of the local noble. There were sufficient untoward incidents to remind the aristocracy of the danger of an empowered common people. For example, after the defeat and death of Richard of York at Sandal (see page 46), one chronicler reported on the fate of the captured Earl of Salisbury:

1 The Earl of Salisbury was taken alive, and led by the ... Duke of Somerset to the castle of Pomfret [Pontefract], and for a great sum of money that he should have paid had grant of his life. But the common people of the country, which loved him not, took him out
5 of the castle by violence and smote off his head.

This is not an isolated incident. In 1469, the Earl of Devon was captured by the commons after the battle of Edgecote and summarily beheaded.

c) Numbers of casualties

If we have grave difficulty in establishing numbers of participants, can we be clearer on casualty figures? The short answer is no. This is hardly surprising, since sources which so wilfully exaggerate numbers of combatants are hardly likely to provide realistic figures for those killed or wounded. We can again use the battle of Towton as an example of the difficulties. Here is a letter written by the Earl of Warwick's brother, George Neville, Bishop of Exeter, to Francesco Coppini, a papal legate who was inclined to favour the Yorkists whenever possible:

1 The king, the valiant Duke of Norfolk, my brother aforesaid and my uncle, Lord Fauconberg, travelling by different routes, finally united with all their companies and armies near the country round York ... That day there was a great conflict, which began with the
5 rising of the sun, and lasted until the tenth hour of the night, so great was the pertinacity and boldness of the men, who never heeded the possibility of a miserable death. Of the enemy who fled, great numbers were drowned in the river near the town of Tadcaster, eight miles from York, because they themselves had

10 broken the bridge to cut our passage that way, so that none could
   pass, and a great part of the rest who got away who gathered in the
   said town and city, were slain and so many dead bodies were seen
   as to cover an area six miles long by three broad and about four
15 furlongs. In this battle eleven lords of the enemy fell, including the
   Earl of Devon, the Earl of Northumberland, Lord Clifford and
   Neville with some cavaliers; and from what we hear from persons
   worthy of confidence, some 28,000 persons perished on one side
   and the other.

We also have a letter from William Paston and Thomas Playter to John
Paston I.

1 Please you to know ... such tidings as my Lady of York (mother of
  Edward IV) hath by a letter of credence under the sign manual of
  our sovereign lord King Edward, which letter came unto our said
  lady this same day ... at 11 clock, and was seen and read by me,
5 William Paston. First, our sovereign lord hath won the field, and
  upon the Monday next after Palm Sunday he was received into
  York with great solemnity and processions ... On the contrary part
  [i.e. the Lancastrian side] is dead Lord Clifford, Lord Neville,
  Lord Welles, Lord Willoughby, Antony Lord Scales ... and many
10 other gentlemen and commons to the number of 20,000.

Ross is rightly sceptical of such figures, commenting that 'one
chronicler's more sober estimate of 9,000 dead - 10 per cent of the
combatants - is likely to be nearer the mark'. This chronicler is, in fact,
the unknown author of the *Annales rerum Anglicarum*. He was writing 30
years after the events and his strong pro-Neville bias is significant. He
had every reason, perhaps, to exaggerate the numbers killed by the
Yorkist side, but does not seem to have done so. This may be seen
(tentatively) as some indication of his reliability.

   We can, at least, definitely reject any notion that England lost a
generation of fighting men. Ross argues that numbers of dead in the
majority of battles numbered hundreds rather than thousands. There is
no evidence that casualties were such that ordinary village life in the
harsh round of the farming year was compromised by lack of men to
work the fields or harvest the crops. For a noble, of course, death on the
battlefield was always a strong possibility. Even so, there is little
evidence to support the view of those like Hall who argued that noble
family after noble family failed in the male line due to the conflicts of the
Wars of the Roses.

   Of course, it could be argued that rural society was nevertheless
devastated by the various armies as they pillaged the countryside in the
time-honoured manner. Time-honoured in the France of the Hundred
Years War, perhaps: but not in the Wars of the Roses. Armies were
simply not engaged in prolonged sieges or on the march for month after

month. Large-scale battles were often decisive. Kings and pretenders lacked the resources for sustained conflict. The only major example of an army going on the rampage is that led from the north by Margaret of Anjou in the winter of 1460-1. The experience was such that contemporary chroniclers used it to warn of the evil rapaciousness of northerners.

> 1 the northmen ... swept onwards like a whirlwind from the north, and in the impulse of their fury attempted to overrun the whole of England. At this period too, fancying that every thing tended to insure them freedom from molestation, paupers and beggars
> 5 flocked forth from those quarters in infinite numbers ... and universally devoted themselves to spoil and rapine ... they also irreverently rushed, in their unbridled and frantic rage, into churches and the other sanctuaries of God, and most nefariously plundered them of their chalices, books, and vestments ... When
> 10 the priests and the other faithful of Christ in any way offered to make resistance, like so many abandoned wretches as they were, they cruelly slaughtered them in the very churches or church yards ... What do you suppose must have been our fears dwelling here in this island, when every day rumours of this sad nature were
> 15 reaching our ears?

It would clearly be foolish to argue that this was the only case of pillaging in the Wars of the Roses. Henry VII, for example, granted £72. 2s. 4d. to various communities whose grain had been seized by his army on its road to Bosworth field. The threats made by commanders to hang those caught pillaging imply that it was a cause for concern: as do the various safe-conducts to merchants issued from the same quarter. Nevertheless, we can dismiss the contention that sustained pillaging was rife through the period of the Wars. In any case, some parts of England - the south west, East Anglia and areas of the north west - were largely spared the spectacle of battlefield carnage and armies on the march.

d) Impact on the Towns

It is hard to resist the conclusion that towns would have ignored the conflicts if they could. And, even when they could not, they were remarkably successful in avoiding damage or even major expenditure in the face of conflicting demands from the opposing sides. Ross provides the helpful example of the city of Norwich. In 1457, a French attack on the East Anglian coast was expected. Norwich immediately offered to supply 600 men. In 1461, the city grudgingly provided 120 men to fight for Henry VI. The disparity is easily explained. In 1457, the city's trading interests were threatened; in 1461, they were not. In fact, the Lancastrians were not disadvantaged by the lack of men from Norwich:

for various reasons (none of which involved firm political principles), they ended up switching sides and fighting for Edward IV at Towton.

Some towns tended to offer help to whichever army happened to be closest and therefore the greatest potential threat. In 1471, Salisbury kept up a barrage of messengers laden with promises and excuses to Lancastrian and Yorkists alike. Edward IV happened to pass closest to the city, so he was sent a derisory band of 14 men as he made his way to Tewkesbury.

A few towns were markedly more partisan, if not markedly more generous. Richard III was a good and open-handed friend to the city of York, and honoured the town by creating his son, Edward, Prince of Wales in York Minster. The York civic records testify to the city's sorrow on hearing of the king's defeat at Bosworth field:

1 King Richard, late lawfully reigning over us, was, through great treason of the Duke of Norfolk and many others that turned against him, with many other lords and nobility of these north parts, piteously slain and murdered, to the great heaviness of this 5 city.

But York had sent only 80 men to the aid of the king at Bosworth: and those self-same civic records reveal that the first priority had been the defence of the city itself, requiring

that every warden of this city search the inhabitants within his ward, that they have sufficient weapons and array for their defence and the weal of this City.

The city authorities of London threw in their lot with Edward IV when the Lancastrian forces under the Bastard of Fauconberg demanded entry in May 1471. But, again, self-interest rather than loyalty stimulated this unusually committed response. Edward had been generous in granting the city a charter in 1462 which had confirmed various trading privileges and had made some useful additions, such as the right to tax some foreign merchants. He had been exceptionally generous in raising important citizens to the knighthood. Even more to the point, the authorities feared that the Bastard's forces were all too likely to sack the city, and that, as the *Historie of the Arrivall of King Edward IV* put it, there were plenty in London itself who would 'have been right glad of a common robbery, to th'entent they might largely have put their hands in rich men's coffers'.

Whatever the fears of London on this occasion, it is important to note that not one substantial town was subjected to a lengthy siege, and very few were sacked in any of the conflicts of the Wars of the Roses. Indeed, there is no evidence that, despite the periodic nervousness, the trading ventures of the larger towns were directly affected by the Wars.

If it is relatively easy to establish the extent of physical damage to towns, it is much more difficult to work out how the conflicts affected the outlook or attitudes of townspeople. Were they paralysed by anxiety? Did everyday life carry on without hindrance? Were the Wars or rumours of wars merely temporary inconveniences that could be handled by a little deft diplomacy and ready promises on the part of the authorities? Perhaps the best clue to something so abstract is something distinctly concrete - the state of the town defences, and, in particular, the walls. It is a reasonable supposition that anxiety and fear would lead to frantic measures for self-defence: conversely, a town that felt under no meaningful threat would spend little or nothing on the upkeep of defences.

On this basis, our conclusion must be that towns felt reasonably secure. John Gillingham suggests that we do a simple numerical count of those towns receiving grants to finance defensive building. If we compare these over the centuries, we see a significant decline: the total for the fifteenth century is markedly less than those of the previous two centuries. More importantly, the figures for the period of the Wars of the Roses (let us say, the last four decades of the century) are only very slightly up on the figures for the previous four decades: 28 grants as opposed to 26. This would not suggest widespread feelings of insecurity in the towns. Few made real efforts to improve and update defences. Only those facing possible threats from France (like Sandwich or Dover) made concerted and consistent efforts to revitalise defences. This is in stark contrast to the war-torn continent of Europe, where the building of 'bastions' or reinforced platforms for guns within the town defences was a marked feature.

4 The Impact of the Wars of the Roses on Cultural Life

Common sense suggests that devastation and culture do not go well together. There can be exceptions. Certain types of artistic expression can be stimulated by conflict, in the sense that the imaginative life responds to the horror - or even the excitement - of war. However, those aspects of culture that reflect the involvement of whole communities and, frequently, considerable shared expense, are unlikely to flourish in conditions of instability and chronic insecurity. One would not expect, for example, major church building programmes. Similarly, the homes of the aristocracy should reflect the prevailing atmosphere. In times of conflict, we would anticipate the spending of money on extra fortifications. In time of peace, money would be spent on comfort.

It is often argued that the castles and manor houses of the nobility built or improved around the period of the Wars of the Roses place the emphasis on comfort rather than defence. Ross cites Tattershall Castle as an example, and even a cursory glance shows how undefendable such a building would be in the face of determined assault. The builder, Lord

Cromwell, was keen to get as much light as possible into his home: the large windows - particularly those at ground level - were not going to be of much help against cannon-fire. Nor would the 'charming and most unwarlike roof garden' (to use J.R. Lander's phrase). Cromwell clearly felt that cannon-fire was the remotest of possibilities. Having said this, Tattershall was built in 1434 - just before the period of the Wars. Better - if smaller - examples would be Gainsborough Old Hall in Lincolnshire or Great Chalfield Manor in Wiltshire, which date from the 1470s and 1480s and where comfort clearly predominated over defensive capabilities. Before reaching a conclusion on this issue, we ought to consider the different perspective provided by Anthony Goodman. Goodman argues that sieges may have been more frequent than the sources suggest, since the chroniclers were always much more interested in the big, set-piece battles. Commenting on Queen Margaret of Anjou's retreat in 1461, he observes: 'The queen's precipitate and lengthy withdrawal ... may have been hastened by embattled manor-houses and townships along her line of communications, whose inhabitants were desperate to prevent their beasts from being herded off and their meagre winter food stocks from being seized'. Perhaps so, perhaps not. But it is one thing to argue a case on the basis of the limitations of the sources and quite another to fill in the alleged gaps oneself. Tentatively, we should argue that manor-house and castles were less embattled than Goodman suggests, and that the architectural evidence is a reasonably meaningful indicator that the nobility was not strengthening defences and battening down the hatches.

Religious building, similarly, was thriving in the second half of the fifteenth century. There are many possible examples. Long Melford is a spectacular testimony to the wealth of the East Anglian cloth merchants. The illustration below shows details of the inscriptions recording the

The clerestory of Long Melford church

benefactors, whose church was completed in the early 1480s. We might add that there is no sense of despair in the face of violence in the religious architecture of the period. The prevailing style - known to historians of architecture as Perpendicular- emphasised light, height and space rather than the embattled, heavy and dour. In other words, there is a confidence about such architecture that may reflect a belief in the fundamental stability of society. This kind of argument, however, should be taken as no more than a possible indication of a prevailing attitude, rather than proof of it. After all, Henry VI was virtually obsessed by the building of Eton College and King's College, Cambridge. Yet Henry was presiding over chaos rather than light. Perhaps these two foundations reflect instead that king's desire to escape from a reality made harsher by his own failings.

It would be very helpful if we could recover something of the popular culture of the period. What few sources we have do not reveal an obsession with civil war. As for the nobility, it is possible to glean some information from inventories (lists of possessions made after death). Sir John Paston - of that troubled Norfolk family - did not simply have books about law and knighthood or of religious devotion: he also had several that reflect at least some opportunity for leisure, including romances, histories and books about playing chess.

The general tenor of the evidence therefore suggests that the period of the Wars of the Roses by no means marked a decline in cultural life or an obsession with safety, defence and possible death to the exclusion of all else.

5 The Economic Impact of the Wars of the Roses

We have already seen that the Wars did not devastate the countryside. Everyday life - the life of farm and village - was at the mercy of the weather, but not of the Wars. The same is true of the country's commercial life. Roughly nine-tenths of English export was cloth and wool. This trade was only affected when Calais, the chief export market for wool, fell into the hands of rebels. This happened, for example, when the Yorkists held the town in the face of a Lancastrian siege from October 1460 to June 1461. But commerce was dislocated only temporarily. The trade depression from roughly 1450 to the mid 1470s was caused, not by civil war, but primarily by such issues as the loss of Normandy and Gascony (see pages 63-4), failure to curb piracy (which upset England's trading partners), Burgundian embargoes on English cloth, and the like. The support Edward IV received from the City of London in 1471 reflected the hope that he would prove to be much more interested than Henry VI in the city's trade. By and large, the City's decision was a shrewd one. Trade figures show a marked improvement towards the end of Edward's reign. And in some ways, of course, military conflict can improve trade. The manufacture or import of weapons and the cloth trade - for the making of uniforms or the ribbons of allegiance known as 'bends' - were stimulated by the needs of the armies.

6 Conclusion

Philippe de Commynes - an astute diplomat who served the courts of Burgundy and France - was convinced that England was the country in which the ordinary people suffered least from the ravages of war. Disaster and misfortune, he argued, fell only on those who made war - the nobles and their soldiers. There is some truth in his comments. As we have seen, the impact of the Wars on the life of the country at large - its agriculture, its towns, its peasantry - was limited. Cities were not subjected to interminable sieges, the countryside was not ravaged by foraging armies (with the odd but painful exception) and towns were not interrupting trade in the panic to build new defences. One must not forget, however, that the Wars significantly worsened the already parlous state of law and order in the reign of Henry VI. But Commynes exaggerates somewhat the impact on the nobility. There were indeed many casualties among the upper nobility as a direct result of the conflict - through death in the battlefield, or through execution shortly afterwards. We need only remember Somerset and Northumberland at the first battle of St Albans, Richard of York at Sandal, Warwick at Barnet and so on. Nor must we forget the deaths of the kings Henry VI and Richard III, Henry's son Edward, Prince of Wales, or the Princes in the Tower. But only eight noble families (ten if one includes Lancaster and York) were extinguished as a result of the conflicts. A failure to beget male heirs was far more likely to bring a line to an end than death at the point of a sword.

Ross has argued that the political influence of the aristocracy was 'severely reduced as a direct consequence of the Wars of the Roses'. Perhaps we might quibble about the word 'direct'. Edward IV continued to rely heavily on his nobility, even if he did make great use of his new power-blocs like the Woodvilles or the Herberts. Henry VII seems to have deliberately sought to curb noble power, but this is as likely to reflect the attitudes and personality of the king as it is to be a legacy of the Wars themselves. Curb the nobility, however, he certainly did. He succeeded in making loyal service at court the hallmark of status, rather than the possession of massive ancestral lands and draughty castles.

In the longer term, the Wars of the Roses created an attitude of mind which increased the power of the king. Edward IV had been very much the effective, traditional monarch, strong where Henry VI had been weak (in other words, in all aspects of the kingly art). The stability he was able to engender after 1471 genuinely impressed his contemporaries and no doubt made all the greater the contrast with his predecessor. In this way, the Wars gave an opportunity for an able king to impose or even extend his authority in the knowledge that his subjects had acquired a healthy respect for good order and authority through experiencing the lack of both. As memory faded and propaganda stepped in, the Tudors capitalised on the legacy of the Wars of the Roses by creating a myth of horror and carnage. This legacy of the Wars was none the less real for being, to a considerable extent, a Tudor invention.

Making notes on 'The Impact of the Wars of the Roses'

This chapter divides the theme of 'impact' into three parts: political, social and economic impact. Your notes must reflect this. You will find a number of references to different historians in this chapter, and you should certainly note their contrasting views. Examination boards like historiography, but only where it is used correctly. There is no point in trotting out a quotation from an historian unless it carries with it the weight of a particular interpretation, which you should then proceed to evaluate. Also, remember to point out where the evidence does not permit a firm conclusion.

The headings below reflect very closely the titles of the various sections, since many are already expressed in the form of questions.
1.   Introduction. Notes not needed.
2.   The Political Impact of the Wars of the Roses
2.1   Did the Wars of the Roses damage the theory of kingship?
2.2   Did the Wars damage royal authority and increase the power of the nobility in the long term?
2.3   What impact did the Wars of the Roses have on justice and law and order? Make sure you discuss both Edward IV and Henry VII.
2.4   Did the Wars of the Roses weaken the position of the nobility?
3   The Social Impact of the Wars of the Roses
3.1   What are the varying views on the duration of the Wars?
3.2   How many were involved in the military campaigns? Is there evidence of widespread destruction or disruption?
3.3   What conclusions can we come to on the casualty figures?
3.4   Impact on the towns.
4.   The Impact of the Wars of the Roses on cultural life
4.1   What cultural features will be discussed in this section?
4.2   What evidence does religious and secular building provide?
4.3   What evidence does popular and élite culture provide?
5.   The Economic Impact of the Wars of the Roses
6.   Conclusion

Answering essay questions on 'The Impact of the Wars of the Roses'

The good news is that essay questions on the impact of the Wars are likely to be easier than questions on the causes. This is largely because there is less material to master. Here are some typical questions:

1   'Absolutely devastating': 'Remarkably undisruptive of everyday life'. Which of the two views of the Wars of the Roses do you find most convincing, and why?
2   'The political impact of the Wars of the Roses was massive, but the social impact was negligible.' Comment on this view.
3   To what extent was England seriously affected by the Wars of the Roses?

Hopefully, you would find the division of the chapter into political, social and economic issues of value here. Write plans and opening paragraphs for all three essays.

___

Source-based questions on 'The Impact of the Wars of the Roses'

1 The Impact of Battle
Read the extract from the Crowland Chronicle (page 110), the Bishop of Exeter's letter (page 108), and the letter to John Paston (page 109). Answer the following questions.
a)   What evidence is there of the likely profession of the writer of the Crowland Chronicle? (3 marks)
b)   How might the chronicler's profession have distorted his evidence? (2 marks)
c)   Assess the reliability of the two letters. Which do you consider to be the most reliable, and why? (7 marks)

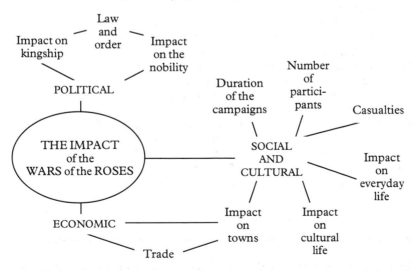

Summary - The Impact of the Wars of the Roses

CHAPTER 6

The Government of Edward IV and Richard III

1 Introduction

One of the problems of using a word like 'government' when discussing fifteenth-century England is that its modern meaning is misleading in the extreme. It conjures up images of corridors of power, bureaucracy, civil servants, commissions, policies, ministers of state, executive departments and a nucleus of power at a place called 'Whitehall'. Most of this is unhelpful baggage, and should be discarded forthwith. Whitehall, perhaps, sounds as if it might be derived from the remoter past - a white hall? - and this is true enough. In fact, Whitehall Palace was a residence of Henry VIII's court from the mid 1530s, and so even this is irrelevant to our discussion of the Yorkists.

Hopefully, previous chapters have equipped readers to spot the potentially anachronistic use of words like 'government'. The image of government in the fifteenth century is something personal beyond the worst nightmare of an officious lover of committees. The king was at its heart: in a very real sense, the government was his.

Having said what government was not, what can we offer as a definition? Briefly, it can be seen as the means whereby the king's authority was imposed over the country. This will therefore involve a discussion of the king's methods of securing his own power through his relations with the political nation, through his economic policies and through his supervision of law and order. It will also be necessary to look at the implications for his domestic affairs of the king's foreign policies.

Students facing examination questions on this period are unlikely to be asked to discuss both the causes of the Wars of the Roses and Yorkist government in one essay. Both themes, of course, shed light on each other. Although this chapter can be read independently of its predecessors, earlier chapters will certainly provide evidence that is relevant to the issues to be discussed below.

2 'New Monarchy'

We have already had cause to comment that history is basically an historian's attempt to impose order on the past. Sometimes, it seems more of an imposition than others. In this case, we are faced with a concept - that of 'New Monarchy' - which has secured a place in the historian's vocabulary and of which we are, therefore, obliged to make use in our analysis of the government of the Yorkist kings.

A brief history of the concept might be helpful. In his *Short History of the English People* (1874), the historian J.R. Green argued that a new monarchy had grown up in the second reign of Edward IV. Allegedly, that king and his successors exploited the curbing of noble power as a result of the Wars of the Roses to build a system in which the king's will triumphed over the traditional liberties of England: in other words, a despotism was founded. Green's basic assumptions were subsequently modified in a number of ways. Some writers have wished to discard 'New Monarchy' altogether; others have wished to argue that it is meaningful only as a result of Henry VIII's policies; others have identified it with Henry VII; and some have seen the increase of royal power as a Europe-wide phenomenon. For those who wish to pursue the wayward course of New Monarchy historiography, Anthony Goodman's short book *The New Monarchy: England 1471-1534* provides an excellent introduction. For our purposes, we simply need to recognise that it is a slippery concept which we must attempt to corner before we can assess its validity. What follows is an attempt to outline in summary the features that have been thought to be a part of 'New Monarchy'. It has to be said that some historians would argue that it is possible to accept the validity of the concept even if a number of these features are absent. This is true enough, but it could equally be argued that their absence would certainly compromise the concept's value to the study of the period.

Briefly, then, we can argue that, for a New Monarchy to be new at all, it has to be significantly different from traditional monarchy. It should, therefore, contain some or all of the following elements:

a) The power of the king will have increased significantly at the expense of the nobility.
b) This will have been accompanied by increased centralisation of power. For example, the traditional near-autonomy of the regions remote from London will have diminished significantly.
c) To complement the previous criterion, law and order will have been subjected increasingly to central direction and the rôle of the nobility therein will have been reduced.
d) The systems of government - such as revenue collection - will have been improved. This will have involved both the establishment of new systems and an increased efficiency: in other words, bureaucratisation.

It is best to make it clear at the outset that the present writer finds the concept of New Monarchy of limited value at best. To structure the rest of the chapter around the various aspects of New Monarchy would be rather like designing a building to make it easy to demolish. Instead, we shall examine the reigns under the themes of relations with the political nation (i.e. those with political power), law and order, finance and foreign policy. This will allow us to handle the broader issues of the nature of Yorkist government and to consider the extent to which it was traditional or innovative, while at the same time permitting a discussion of New Monarchy. It might also be argued that a 'model' such as New Monarchy represents a dangerous temptation for the historian. Such models are attractive in that they appear to give a clear structure to the past. But the danger is that the model becomes more important than the past itself. Reality can be distorted to fit the model, and one tends to forget that the model itself is supposedly derived from the past. It should have no independent validity. If we are to say that, for example, the Yorkists kings were not 'New Monarchs', then the danger is that we are in effect criticising their performance against a set of criteria that is actually inappropriate. The fault is ours, not theirs.

3 Edward IV, Richard III and the Political Nation

In Chapter 5, it was argued that there was no significant change in the relationship between king and nobility in the reign of Edward IV. Had the new king wished to alter that relationship, there were real opportunities created by the number of Lancastrian attainders following his victory in 1461 and again in 1471 with the fall of the Nevilles. The king would certainly have increased his own power directly had he chosen to retain for the crown the estates of his Lancastrian adversaries. But he did not. That land was redistributed as patronage in a manner befiting a generous king who presumably saw a strong nobility as a mark of his own power rather than as a threat to it.

Similarly, the defeat of the Nevilles gave Edward the chance to break with the traditional policy of leaving the troubled Marches of Wales and Scotland in the hands of nobles with vice-regal powers. But again he did not. He was more than ready to let his brother, Gloucester, build up a considerable power base in the Western March (of Scotland). In 1483, Richard's effectiveness was further rewarded:

1 the Duke [of Gloucester], being Warden of the West Marches, by his diligent labours ... has subdued a great part of the west borders of Scotland ... to the great surety and ease of the north parts of England ... [The King grants] that the Duke shall have to him and
5 his heirs male [the] Wardenship of the West Marches of England ... And also [the] making and ordaining of the sheriff of the county of Cumberland.

So, not only is the Wardenship being made hereditary, but Gloucester's control over law and order is made explicit through his rights over the sheriffs.

It might be tempting to argue that Edward, through generous use of ennoblement, effectively changed the nature of the magnate class and made service to the king the clearest mark of that status. The temptation should be resisted. He did, of course, raise some nobles to magnate status. It is hardly surprising that he should elevate his own brothers and members of his new queen's family. However, he also elevated a number who were not in the higher rank of the nobility - Hastings and Sir William Herbert being the two best examples (see page 74). But this was not part of a conscious policy to use the gentry to replace or to threaten the old-established magnates. If it had been, Edward IV would have been looking for an opportunity to destroy Warwick. But there is no evidence that he was, and, as we know, Warwick self-destructed in a spectacular manner. Thus there seems little option but to see Edward IV as an eminently traditional king whose attitude to his nobility reflected the fact that he had been one of their number. He understood their world view, accepted it, enjoyed their company and controlled them by the force of his considerable personality - much as he would have controlled his retainers and tenants as Earl of March.

As a king beset by plots and rebellion, Richard III benefited, like Edward IV, from the influx of lands forfeited by traitors. To take just one example, the rebellion of 1483 presented him with the estates of the greatest private landowner in the country, the Duke of Buckingham. But, like Edward IV, Richard did not hold on to them as crown land. He distributed them with a keen eye to his political needs. It was not generosity. The king eagerly - and illegally - grabbed the lands of those involved in the 1483 rebellion without waiting for the Acts of Attainder to go through Parliament. What he did with them provoked the outrage of the Crowland chronicler.

1 He distributed all these [lands] amongst his northerners whom he
  had planted in every part of his dominions, to the shame of all the
  southern people who murmured ceaselessly and longed more each
  day for the return of their old lords in place of the tyranny of the
5 present ones.

The evidence cannot quantify the extent of the murmuring and longing, but it certainly confirms that the king did indeed impose outsiders on those parts of the country whose loyalty was most suspect. Let this not be mistaken for some form of 'New Monarchy'-style centralisation of power. It was simply bitter necessity. As was argued in Chapter 4, (see pages 88-9), most of Edward IV's former servants were unwilling to come to terms with the usurpation - and particularly those whose lands were remote from Gloucester's former centre of influence in the north. Their part in the rebellion demonstrated all too clearly that Richard could not trust them. And so, Richard found himself relying on northerners whom he could trust and on a very small group of great magnates whose trustworthiness was less certain.

Why were there so few great nobles? The answer lies with Richard himself. He had, after all, savaged the Woodvilles, destroyed Hastings and executed the rebel Buckingham. But if it came to a major military campaign in the defence of his throne, then the support of the three remaining magnates would be vital. These men received plentiful patronage from the king, for the simple reason that he could not do without them. They were: Thomas, Lord Stanley (with a massive power-base in the north west); The Earl of Northumberland (with a power-base in the north); John Howard, Duke of Norfolk (with a power-base in East Anglia). Norfolk was a firm supporter of Richard and, indeed, owed his dukedom to him. But Northumberland had no love for the king. He had been his rival in the days when Edward IV had used Richard of Gloucester to control the north. Worse still, Stanley was a devious schemer whose unreliability was compounded by the fact that he was married to Henry Tudor's mother.

Richard might, perhaps, have built up other great magnate factions to offset the dangers inherent in the situation. By and large, he did not. Two possible reasons may be tentatively advanced. First, he could not afford to antagonise the three existing magnates by the introduction of rivals. Second, he lacked the fellow-feeling bred of self-confidence that allowed Edward IV to be generous for generosity's sake to his nobility. For these reasons, Richard was anything but free with ennoblement. As we have seen, Howard was the main beneficiary. There were others - notably, Howard's son, who was made Earl of Surrey, and William, Viscount Berkeley, who was made Earl of Nottingham. This is hardly an impressive number. Nor did Richard promote into the lower peerage. Even those of his supporters who received most patronage - like Sir Richard Ratcliffe and William Catesby - might be given the lands, offices and wealth that became a baron, but they were never given the title. As Ross suggests, this might well reflect their unpopularity as intruders and upstarts. Richard's sensitivity to this issue is well revealed by the severity of his treatment of the unfortunate and unwise William Collingbourne, whose scurrilous rhyme against the king's key agents Ratcliffe, Catesby and Viscount Lovell brought him to a terrible fate. Fabyan's chronicle is not sparing in the details.

1 During this time many gentlemen ... departed over the sea into
France and there allied themselves with the virtuous Prince Henry,
son unto the Earl of Richmond ... one, named William
Collingbourne, was taken [captured] ... [and] cast for sundry
5 treasons and for a rhyme [in] derision of the king and his council,
as follows:
   The cat, the rat, and Lovell our dog
   Ruleth all England under a hog.
... For this ... he was put to the most cruel death on Tower Hill
10 where, for him, was made a new pair of gallows upon which, after
he had hanged a short season, he was cut down, being alive, and his
bowels ripped out of his belly and cast into the fire there by him,
and lived till the butcher put his hand into the bulk of his body;

insomuch that he said in the same instant, 'O Lord Jesu, yet more
15 trouble', and so died to the great compassion of many people.

It would seem, therefore, that Richard III's relationships with his
nobility were inevitably coloured by widespread dislike of his
usurpation. The great magnates benefited from his patronage simply
because they were great magnates. Unlike his successor, Henry VII,
Richard III never felt sufficiently secure to bestow patronage only when
it was earned by conspicuous loyalty and good service. His death at
Bosworth field is a testimony to the failure of his relations with at least
one of these magnates, since it was the treason of the Stanley family that
led directly to his death (see page 90). Northumberland appears to have
played little part in the battle. Whether this was due to the positioning of
the forces under his command (he was in charge of the rearguard) or to
some reluctance to commit himself, we have no way of knowing.
Contemporary sources suggest that Richard may have suspected
disloyalty.

More positively, we should draw attention to one innovation in
Richard III's dealings with the nobility. Instead of following the usual
practice of entrusting the north of England to a powerful magnate, he
chose to install a Council of the North. In effect, this was a branch of the
royal council responsible for good order in the Scottish borders. Its
president was the one magnate the king felt he could trust - Norfolk,
who was not himself a major landowner in the region. We do not have a
list of council members, but it is likely that Norfolk was assisted by
well-connected local nobles. What we must not do is argue that this new
council represents increased centralisation of authority. We have -
needless to say - no record of Richard's intentions, but it is likely enough
that he employed a conciliar solution because he could not trust the
obvious regional magnate, Northumberland. If the king had intended
some sort of administrative innovation, it is likely that he would have
established a similar body for Wales. But he did not, even though there
was a precedent for such a body. Edward IV had set up a Council in the
Marches of Wales - or, rather, it had developed out of that king's desire
for his young son Edward to have his household based in the Marches at
Ludlow castle.

Clearly, then, to apply the New Monarchy concept to the Yorkist
kings' relations with the nobility would be an imposition indeed.
However, it does seem reasonable to argue that Henry VII's entrapment
of the nobility in his web of recognisances (see page 101) was a sign of a
changing relationship in which the king's power increased and the
independence of the noble diminished. Although it is beyond the scope
of this book to establish where, when and if ever New Monarchy is a
useful concept, it appears justifiable to see Henry VII's increasing
authority as a sign of its relevance.

4 Law and Order under Edward IV

a) Retaining

Having in the previous section discussed the relationship between king and nobility, it makes sense to start our discussion of law and order by looking at the Yorkists' treatment of the vexed problem of retaining. It was often assumed - and with reason - that the prolific granting of livery and badges by nobles to their followers led directly to quarrels, quarrels to violence, and both to the courts where the retainers duly practised the corrupt art of bribing and intimidating juries ('maintenance'). For fuller definitions of livery, maintenance and the related practice of embracery, see page 36.

Charles Ross has argued that it was the 'crucial failure' of Edward IV's government that he should fail to launch any real onslaught on livery and maintenance. Perhaps so: but the failure is not a surprising one. It was argued on page 101 that Edward's very real successes lay in the ability to curb his nobility through the force of his energetic personality. He did not see powerful nobles with a full complement of retainers as a threat, but rather as a reflection of his own power and a useful addition to it should he need to call upon their armed support. This is not to say that Edward failed to make the right noises about the potential dangers of retaining. At the start of his reign in 1461, he prohibited the giving of liveries without the king's express and specific permission. And in 1468, a statute made retaining itself an illegal act, save in the case of domestic servants and legal advisers. However, as J.G. Bellamy has pointed out, the wording was ambiguous. It was possible to interpret a clause permitting retaining for 'loyal service' in a number of ways, and not merely in the case of lawyers or servants. But the main point is that the king never enforced the statute. So, what was it for? Perhaps it should be seen as a gesture to the Commons or even the justices of the peace to signify the king's interest in law and order. The nobles themselves clearly saw it as an exercise in public relations, and treated it accordingly. Chief Justice Hussey was clearly scandalised by their behaviour when he witnessed an oath-taking in Star Chamber. The nobles took the appropriate oaths, agreeing to abide by the statute and refrain from taking retainers. So far, so good. But, almost unbelievably, they then illegally took on retainers - also in Star Chamber, and also on oath!

b) Justice

We have had cause to argue that the king's relations with the nobility were traditional and generally characterised by a mutual respect. Edward was not going to deprive the nobles of the control of local law and order which was part and parcel of their rôle and status. Nor was he going to enquire too closely into the way in which the law was manipulated - or ignored - to serve their own ends. But there was one important proviso. Their actions should not call into question the king's authority, either directly through ignoring a specific command or indirectly through gross violations of the king's peace or rebellion. What did the Edward do when faced with such affronts to his dignity and safety?

First, he could and did intervene in person. He was particularly conspicuous in cases of treason. This kind of approach suited Edward's personality. Exhibiting his energy and considerable presence had, of course, an important political dimension. Early in his first reign, his judicial progresses were effective in sorting out disorder and riot. In 1464, for example, he made his way from Coventry to Worcester and thence to Gloucester, Cambridge and Kent. And, of course, these progresses also impressed on his subjects that they now had the privilege of being ruled by an effective king who would brook no nonsense. The contrast with Henry VI did not need to be made explicit. Similarly, Sir John Paston discovered to his cost that it was not a good idea to ignore the king's personal summons. His brother, Clement Paston, wrote to him on 11 October 1461 in something of a panic.

> 1 Brother, I recommend me to you... Sir, it was told me by right a
>   worshipful man that loveth you right well, and ye him, and ye shall
>   know his name hereafter, but put all things out of doubt he is such
>   a man as will not lie: on the eleventh day of October the King said,
> 5 "We have sent two privy seals to Paston by two yeomen of our
>   chamber, and he disobeyeth them; but we will send him another
>   tomorrow, and by God's mercy an if he come not then he shall die
>   for it. We will make all other men beware by him how they shall
>   disobey our writing."

Paston duly attended the king, and found himself clapped in the Fleet prison for his disobedience.

Of course, the king could not be everywhere. He therefore relied heavily on special commissions of *oyer and terminer* ('hear and determine') to sort out major breakdowns of law and order. Significantly, these were headed by one or several magnates to give them the required prestige: a prestige that could be backed up with armed retainers if required.

The king had a further weapon against treason which did not need common law courts - the constable's court, which operated under the so-called 'law of arms'. This meant that those traitors who were taken on the field of battle, had been conspicuously involved in armed rebellion against the king, or who had reneged on royal pardons, were punished without the usual procedure of indictment and trial by jury.

It is important to recognise that there is something almost

aggressively traditional in the king's methods. Edward's energetic perambulations smack of early medieval kings whose acquaintance with England – and perhaps with kingship itself – was less than perfect, but who intended to make their presence felt. Real innovations in Edward's reign were distinctly limited. It is significant that one was the appointment of a special officer in 1467 to investigate and prosecute those who sought to thwart the power and authority of the king: the crime known as *lèse-majesté*.

Traditional approaches to law and order were not going to curb the equally traditional disorder of English society. Murderers and robbers who had the right magnate connections, or who lived in the remoter parts of England, or whose services were needed by the king, or who were simply sufficiently ruthless, pursued their nefarious ways largely unchecked. The only real defence against them was to hope that their behaviour so annoyed the king that he intervened personally. And the suffering of his less well-connected subjects did not unduly concern him. He was only slightly less generous with his pardons than Henry VI.

5 Law and Order under Richard III

There is an ambivalence about Richard III's approach to justice that reflects the contradictions in his personality and in his reign. He is the loyal younger brother who yet deposes (and probably encompasses the death of) his brother's children; the man who shows unmistakable signs of piety, and who yet – it is alleged – accuses his god-fearing mother of adultery for his own political ends: and a king who seizes the land of opponents without due process of law but who nevertheless appears to have genuinely wished to spread the benefits of law to all his subjects.

How strong is the case that Richard was indeed concerned that all – including the poor – should have access to justice? There is little to go on by way of Richard's actions given the brevity of his reign, so we are forced to rely on less tangible evidence. If words alone are a sufficient testimony, then the king was very concerned indeed. Here is an extract from a proclamation in Kent following the 1483 rebellion.

1 the king's highness is fully determined to see due administration of justice throughout this his realm ... and to reform, punish and subdue all extortions and oppressions in the same. And for the cause wills that, at his coming now into his county of Kent, every 5 person dwelling within the same that finds himself grieved, oppressed or unlawfully wronged make a bill of his complaint and put it to his highness ... For his grace is utterly determined all his true subjects shall live in rest and quiet and peaceably enjoy their lands, livelihoods and goods according to the laws of this his land.

This is impressive as far as it goes, and there is some limited corroboration of this publicly-stated interest in justice. For example, Richard designated and rewarded John Harrington as clerk of the council of requests and supplications, which gave access to the law for those who could not otherwise afford it. Significantly, the grant of £20 per year to Harrington is accompanied by a comment on his good service:

> especially in the custody, registration and expedition of bills, requests and supplications of poor persons.

The concern for the poor is echoed by comments made at the time by John Rous in the so-called *Rous Rolls* (a history of the Earls of Warwick, one in Latin and the other in English). Rous commented:

> 1 The most mighty prince Richard by the grace of God king of England and of France and lord of Ireland ... all avarice [greed for money] set aside, ruled his subjects in his realm full commendably, punishing offenders of his laws, especially extortioners and
> 5 oppressors of his commons, and cherishing tho[se] that were virtuous; by the which discreet guiding he got great thank of God and love of all his subjects rich and poor and great laud [praise] of the people.

However, only the most unwary would take Rous at face value. He was a committed Yorkist while the Yorkists were in power, but altered his work once Henry VII came to the throne. Out went the praise of Richard III (and of Edward IV for good measure): in came a ludicrous portrait of Richard as a remarkably hairy new-born with a full set of teeth and a predisposition for evil. It is therefore very tempting to dismiss Rous's praise along with his disfavour. But perhaps we should still draw attention to the way in which he singles out Richard's treatment of the poor. It might tentatively be suggested that this was more specific than one would expect of the standard fulsome eulogy.

So, we are left with that contradiction: the concerned monarch and the ruthless usurper. In fact, the contradiction is relatively easy to resolve. Richard III was happy enough to further the cause of justice for all with the proviso that it did not interfere with his own interests. To call this hypocrisy is unhelpful. It should be seen as a reflection of the importance Richard attached to kingship. After all, his path to the throne was strewn with corpses, vanishing nephews and broken promises. Since that kingship had cost him and others so dear, he was going to take his duties seriously. And one duty was to act as the fount of justice. So it seems that he did just that, as far as his brief and troubled reign permitted him.

In conclusion, then, it should be clear that the New Monarchy model is inappropriate in any discussion of the Yorkist kings and law and order. There is nothing by way of centralisation or bureaucratisation. Instead, we see men who were not born to the royal title exploiting as far as possible the traditional methods of kingship. They were energetic and prepared to intervene personally where necessary. But they were equally content to rely on nobles to fulfil their rôle as agents of the king.

6 Finance under Edward IV: the Revenue of the King

Most financial systems are based on the handling of incoming and outgoing money, and that of the medieval king was no exception. What, then, were the outgoings? First, there were the expenses of running the royal household in all its necessary opulence and luxury. Then there was the expenditure connected with the king's obligation to defend the kingdom: the royal castles, the garrison at Calais, salaries of the wardens of the Marches. Other fees and salaries included those of the 'departments of state' - especially Chancery and the Exchequer - the law courts and the officers of the household. Members of the royal family needed to be looked after. There were also the numerous gifts to be made as part of the patronage system, the donations to the Church and so on. This was the 'ordinary' expenditure, and was supposedly met out of the king's income. The king was, then, expected to 'live of his own'.

The incomings were of four main types. First, there was the income of the crown lands. Second, there were the various feudal dues (see page 22), such as reliefs, the king's rights of wardship (or the sale thereof), fees paid by widows to remarry and so on. Third, the king collected customs duties, levied mainly on the export of wool, cloth, and hides, and the import of wines. Strictly speaking, these customs duties had to be granted by Parliament. In practice, they tended to be treated as a right: Edward IV collected them from the beginning of his reign, and bothered to obtain the required Act only in 1465. Finally, the king took the profits from the legal system, of which fines made up the greatest part.

In times of emergency, the king could not be expected to rely upon this 'ordinary' revenue. Extraordinary revenue could be obtained by taxation, but, as we saw on page 33, taxes could only be collected with the consent of, and as specified by, Parliament. Usually, taxation took the form of a 'fifteenth and tenth'. This was not an income tax, but was supposedly based on the value of a person's movable goods: one-fifteenth of their value in country areas, one-tenth in towns. Its value was limited by the fact that the assessments upon which it was based were hopelessly out of date. The king might also ask, beg, request, demand or extort a straightforward loans from his wealthier subjects depending on how much he frightened them. The Church was also a possible source of revenue. Convocation - the parliament of the Church - could normally be relied on to respond positively to the king's need for war taxation.

7 The Finances of the Yorkist Kings

a) The Collection of Revenue: Exchequer *versus* Chamber

When Edward IV seized the throne in 1461, the king's revenue was dealt with by the Exchequer. Its time-honoured procedures most definitely did not exploit those revenues to the full. The Exchequer's system of collecting revenue from the king's lands is a case in point. It farmed out the lands in return for a fixed rent: and the farmer simply kept the profits above that rent for himself. One of its main functions was to audit accounts, but its processes were interminable. In fact, the Exchequer had serenely ignored the many improvements in estate management made by the nobility. In particular, magnates increasingly used those lesser nobility who were educated in common law, accounting methods and property deeds as receiver-generals to control and maximise the revenue from their lord's estates. Unlike the Exchequer officials - who never left Westminster - they were constantly supervising the estates from the vantage point of a horse.

Sometimes, it was an advantage for Edward IV to have been brought up as a magnate rather than as a prospective king. He was familiar with the relatively efficient system of receiver-generals, and sensibly concluded that they should replace the farmers beloved of the Exchequer. And so, with a few exceptions, land that belonged or fell to the king was to be administered by receivers. It would be tempting to argue that this resulted in much more revenue flowing into the king's coffers. Common sense dictates that there would have been a distinct improvement, although there are no figures to substantiate it. And, of course, the king's generosity in handing on land forfeited by attainder to his own magnates to some extent blunted the impact of the reforms.

Of greater significance was Edward's further reduction of the rôle of the Exchequer. Although it was not abolished (retaining, for example, its legal responsibility for investigating corruption among officials), many of its financial functions were transferred to the royal household itself - in fact, to the king's private apartment, the chamber (see page 31). Revenues from land, from vacant bishoprics, taxation as approved by Parliament, loans of various types, and customs revenue therefore went directly to the chamber.

The great advantage from Edward's point of view was that his financial administration was immediately to hand. He could supervise the work of his officers directly, could give personal instructions by word of mouth if necessary, and could see that those instructions were carried out with all due dispatch. Financial policy became tangible. So did the actual money - sitting in the king's coffers in the chamber. Spending could be monitored. And the king could observe the effect of reforms himself. Certainly the king's finances benefited directly from the chamber system. In particular, he could and did make sure that there was sufficient cashflow to meet the expenses of the household. And the general outlook of the chamber was far more go-ahead than that of the Exchequer. Its business was to augment the king's revenue, rather than simply to handle it.

The usefulness of the chamber system is revealed by Richard III's deliberate reintroduction of it as soon as the early uncertainties and turmoil of the first months of his reign had abated. The new king clearly understood its potential as an agent for increasing royal revenue. One memorandum (undated, but possibly from October 1484) makes a number of suggestions to improve the chamber's revenue collection. In particular, there is a clear statement of the need for professionalism and appropriate legal training for those who worked as stewards of the king's property.

1 Also where that lords, knights and esquires, many of them not lettered be made stewards of the king's livelihood in divers countries [counties], they taking great fines and rewards of the king's tenants ... to the king's hurt and poverishing of his said
5 tenants, and also wanting cunning and discretion to order and direct the said livelihood lawfully ... Therefore it is thought that learned men in the law were most profitable to be stewards...

Does the chamber system of finance fit the New Monarchy concept? Do we see increased centralisation and bureaucratisation? On the face of it, we do. After all, the reduction in the rôle of the Exchequer meant that the system was centralised in the chamber. But this is emphatically not new. It is simply a traditional and reinvigorated system - and surely the phrase 'New Monarchy' demands more than that. As for bureaucratisation, there is, as we have seen, an increased emphasis on professionalism which might be taken as an indicator of a Yorkist willingness to employ 'new men' (perhaps of middle-class origin) as their agents. This view can be rejected. There is no evidence that significant numbers of the middle-class were elevated to positions of authority within the financial administration. It is true, however, that Edward exploited the increasing education of the lower nobility (the gentry) by using them within the household and as receivers or surveyors. He was, in fact, making less use of the clergy as civil servants. On the other hand, the comments in Richard III's memorandum do indeed place an emphasis on the need for educated servants, with the implication that these are more likely to be legal professionals than nobles. But then the comments are limited to the role of receivers, and there is no reason to assume that a noble with the right legal training would be rejected. In any case, it is impossible, given the brevity of Richard's reign, to detect any meaningful shift in the social status of royal servants within the financial system. Where we do have some evidence, it suggests that Richard retained many of his brother's receivers and that they were established household men.

None of this amounts to the bureaucratisation and centralisation beloved of New Monarchy. The most important point on the Yorkist system of chamber finance is simply that it worked well: so well, in fact, that the shrewdest of shrewd kings, Henry VII, adopted it after an initial period of flirtation with a restored Exchequer.

b) The Crown becomes Solvent

Edward IV certainly had problems in making ends meet in his first reign, despite his reforms of chamber finance. This meant that he avoided - or abused - his actual legal rights to raise ready cash. In 1464, he requested a so-called 'gratuitous subsidy' from the clergy on the occasion of the Pope's appeal for a crusade. The Pope saw little of the funds collected by the royal agents. He also made money out of his own grants of land and office. In that same year, he demanded a payment of one-quarter of the annual value of the grant (so long as the grant was worth more than 10 marks a year). The king's shortage of ready money was not untypical. The monarchs of late medieval England were almost constantly in debt and found it difficult to meet the wage bill for their own officials. What is unusual is that Edward IV found it relatively easy to raise loans, both from the merchants of London and from Italian bankers. This readiness to lend is a testimony to the way in which Edward's energetic financial policies (and his own evident interest in commerce) had impressed hard-nosed men of business.

Indeed, the king was virtually solvent by 1475. How had he managed it? First, there was the increased income from the royal estates: although one has to accept that the king's willingness to grant out the lands he acquired from Lancastrians and their supporters meant that this revenue was substantially less than it might have been. Second, he attempted to exploit effectively his feudal dues - rights of wardship, relief payments and the like - although his success was, perhaps, somewhat limited. Ross applauds the king for his recognition of the problem, but doubts whether the enforcement was particularly effective. A report in 1471 identified the failure of tenants on the Duchy of Lancaster lands to make the payment they should on inheriting their property, but a further report 8 years later could identify no improvement. Third, he was able to increase revenue from customs through a vigorous campaign against pirates (who had preyed on merchants, thus reducing the customs dues the latter would have paid). He also appointed surveyors to curb evasion of such dues. More significant is a genuine increase in foreign trade, which of course improved customs revenue markedly (see page 114). The king can take some of the credit here, since treaties with France (the Treaty of Picquigny, 1475) and with Burgundy (1478) eased burdensome restrictions and allowed trade in cloth and wine to expand impressively. The relative tranquillity of England also assisted the recovery of trade. Indeed, the king was happy enough to take on the rôle of merchant himself, importing and exporting a variety of commodities. He was also prepared to lease the ships of the navy to London merchants whenever possible. However, it would be an exaggeration to portray Edward as a kind of merchant-king, bursting with entrepreneurial spirit and a sense of mercantile mission. Many of his policies on trade were encompassed by purely subsidiary clauses of treaties made for political reasons, and his willingness to listen to London commercial interests as voiced through Parliament was stimulated by self-interest and the need for support.

A further cause of the crown's solvency was a direct result of foreign policy: the pension of 50,000 gold crowns per year from the French king as agreed at the Treaty of Picquigny.

Contemporary observers were suitably impressed by the king's apparent financial acumen. Here are the comments of the Crowland chronicler.

1 he [Edward IV] turned all his thoughts to the question, how he might in future collect an amount of treasure worthy of his royal station out of his own substance, and by the exercise of his own energies. ... Throughout all ports of the kingdom he appointed
5 inspectors of the customs, men of remarkable shrewdness, but too hard, according to general report, upon the merchants. The king himself, also, having procured merchant ships, put on board of them the finest wools, cloth, tin, and other productions of the kingdom, and, like a private individual living by trade, exchanged
10 merchandise for merchandise ... The revenues of vacant prelacies which, according to Magna Carta, cannot be sold, he would only part with out of his hands at a stated sum ... He also examined the registers and rolls of Chancery, and exacted heavy fines from those whom he found to have intruded and taken possession of estates
15 without prosecuting their rights in form required by law ... added to which, there was the yearly tribute of ten thousand pounds due from France ... All these particulars, in the course of a very few years, rendered him an extremely wealthy prince ... not one of his predecessors was at all able to equal his remarkable achievements.

Although one can quibble at the king's effectiveness as a financial policy-maker, his achievement remains real enough. He had succeeded in converting the bankrupt kingdom and empty treasury of Henry VI into the first debt-free English kingdom with a healthy treasury for two centuries.

c) Richard III and Finance

Richard III was accused by the Crowland chronicler of a 'rapid consumption of that very rich treasure which King Edward thought he had left behind him'. In fact, Edward's military expenses on conflict with France and Scotland in the last few years of his reign had considerably reduced the surplus. And Richard had to pay for his brother's lavish funeral and his own equally lavish coronation. Cashflow was therefore an immediate problem. His policies were virtually identical to those of Edward. We have already seen that he revived chamber finance, and he benefited greatly from the vast additions to the crown lands through forfeiture. Like his brother, he was willing to grant out the forfeited land to supporters, but insisted on being paid an annual rent for the land. He also continued Edward's policy of recovering lapsed feudal dues. But his financial situation early in 1485 was such that he needed to request loans from his greater subjects. Commissioners were sent out to the counties with letters requesting specific sums. A number of these letters were addressed to named individuals, but the choice of most recipients - or victims - was left to the discretion of the commissioners. There is no exact precedent for this in Edward IV's reign, although the former had demanded so-called 'benevolences' to fund military ventures in 1474-5 and in 1481. These were not loans, since Edward had no intention, unlike Richard, of repaying the money raised. It seems that Richard III's requests for loans were markedly unsuccessful.

Any conclusion on the financial policies of the Yorkist kings should emphasise their similarity. Both kings were energetic in supervising the chamber system of finance, and both sought to exploit traditional sources of revenue. If Edward IV is seen to be more successful than his brother, then it must not be forgotten that Richard III had just two years on the throne. Had he triumphed at Bosworth field, it is possible that his energy and commitment might have returned the crown to its unusual position of solvency.

8 Yorkist Foreign Policy - an Introduction

Although foreign policy is not one of the main themes of this book, it would be most unwise to ignore it. To do so would be to assume that England and its monarchs were somehow immune from the ambitions and troubles of their European neighbours, or that the English kings' ambitions and troubles never concerned Europe. This is clearly untrue. After all, England was not even an island. Its border with Scotland was, as we know, an area fraught with tension. Also, the French origin of the post-conquest English monarchs was reflected in their continuing claims to the throne of France, in their territories in France itself, and in the prolonged struggles of the Hundred Years War. Trade and foreign policy of course went hand-in-hand. Like dynastic marriage, trade was a useful weapon in relations between nations.

What were the general aims of English foreign policy? This is a necessary question, although 'general aims of English foreign policy' is rather a grand - and potentially anachronistic - phrase. There was little by way of the trappings of modern diplomacy, such as resident ambassadors, swift lines of communication, professional staff and agreed objectives. Foreign policy was accepted to be the king's preserve, with the accompanying assumption that his kingdom was his personal property. If the king wanted to go to war in defence of his interests - or to extend that personal property - then to war the country went. War, as long as it was carried on abroad, was not generally seen as a misfortune. It was thought to be both a legitimate method of achieving one's ends and an opportunity for the king and nobility to demonstrate their chivalry and military prowess.

However, the king's apparently absolute authority over foreign policy was tempered by the fact that he needed the support of the majority of the political nation. Parliament would need to grant taxes, and the nobility would need to honour its feudal obligations to provide soldiers for the armies. There was certainly the expectation that the king's foreign policies should offer some benefit to the kingdom as a whole. In particular, English merchants would hope for some meaningful return.

Within this general framework, there were certain aims and assumptions that were common to all English kings of the late Middle Ages. The first assumption was that the King of France was their greatest rival, and that France offered the best opportunity for glory or booty (and preferably both). Traditionally, the English kings would look to the duchies of Brittany and Burgundy for allies against the French king, since both felt at various times under threat from him. In return, France could often rely on the support of the so-called 'Auld alliance' with Scotland, which rested on the latter's fear of her more powerful southern neighbour.

In addition, the Yorkist kings had other specific aims. Given the circumstances of their usurpations, it was inevitable that they should fear the possibility that foreign monarchs would seek to destabilise England by supporting pretenders. The other side of the coin is that Edward IV and Richard III would look to international recognition to help secure their dynasties at home.

A mere description of the foreign policies of Edward IV and Richard III would yield little of historical value. Historians - and examiners - generally prefer an analysis which attempts to assess success and failure. And, perhaps, the most meaningful way of doing this is to compare those policies to the monarch's aims as identified in the preceding paragraphs.

9 The Foreign Policy of Edward IV

Edward IV showed considerable shrewdness in the early years of his reign in his dealings with France and Scotland. It was to Scotland that Margaret of Anjou and Henry VI fled after their defeat at Towton, and to Louis XI of France (her kinsman) that the vigorous Margaret looked for further military assistance. Faced with Scottish-backed Lancastrian incursions into northern England, Edward might be criticised for lack of commitment and personal involvement. On the other hand, letting magnates like Warwick handle the immediate military problems was eminently sensible. It gave the king the opportunity to strengthen his hold on the south and on the machinery of government - a success which was useful in foreign policy terms, since it impressed on his French rival the fact that Edward was not going to be easy to destabilise. It also gave the English king the chance to concentrate on supervising the conduct of foreign policy. This, he could hardly do if he were embroiled in northern sieges and skirmishes. His efforts were duly rewarded by a truce with France in 1463 (in which Louis explicitly renounced any assistance to Henry VI). And, in June 1464, his personal negotiations with the Scots led to a 15-year truce.

So far, then, Edward IV's foreign policies appear eminently successful. His dynasty was now recognised by his fellow monarchs, and all he needed to cement that recognition was a suitable marriage into an appropriate royal family. But then, of course, he married Elizabeth Woodville in the spring of 1464 (see page 74). However, it would be quite wrong to argue that this misalliance actually jeopardised his position abroad, although it did little for Edward's reputation as a statesman. In fact, tensions between Louis and the duchies of Burgundy and Brittany (who saw the French king as a threat to their traditional independence) meant that all three parties were keen for an alliance of some sort with England. Warwick was keen to secure an alliance with France, but Edward preferred to adopt the standard anti-French posture by seeking treaties with Brittany and Burgundy. By the summer of 1468, France was ringed by those three adversaries and Edward was, to all intents and purposes, preparing for an invasion of France. The relationship with Charles of Burgundy was confirmed by the duke's marriage with Edward's sister, Margaret.

In the event, nothing came of the proposed invasion as the French king managed to detach both dukes from their treaties with England. Ross feels that it is unlikely that Edward was unduly disappointed by the loss of the chance to invade France. This is a sensible conclusion, since, by the terms of his treaties, he clearly intended to provide only limited assistance to his allies. In any case, the closeness of his relationship with Burgundy and Brittany was rebuilt almost immediately, and France was isolated diplomatically once more.

There was, however, one danger implicit in Edward IV's attitude towards France. Louis had every incentive to support the Lancastrians, and it was his support that played a crucial part in the successful invasion of England that led to the Readeption (see page 80). Edward did perhaps underestimate the wiliness of Louis, who may well have persuaded Warwick of the feasibility of an alliance with Margaret of Anjou. Edward may also have underestimated the extent to which

Warwick had committed himself to a French alliance. But then he could not have anticipated the depth of the treason of Warwick and, in particular, Clarence. The loss of his throne was not directly attributable to his foreign policy, but it did not help.

Following the recovery of his throne in 1471, it might be expected that Edward would seek a swift revenge against the French king. But 'swift' was not a word in the vocabulary of his likely allies, the cool and calculating Charles of Burgundy and the vacillating Francis of Brittany. It was July 1474 before the Treaty of London brought in Burgundy as a military ally in a French invasion: Edward's goal was the French crown. In May 1475, Brittany joined the alliance. Meanwhile, Edward had successfully secured a long-term truce and a marriage alliance with his likely adversary James III of Scotland.

The king's preparation for invasion was impressive. He secured taxes from a Parliament which did not entirely trust his good faith in engaging in a military campaign. He also persuaded the wealthy nobility to provide further funds through the non-returnable 'benevolence' (see page 133). In all probability, the army which left for Calais in 1475 was the largest (if not the most experienced) to invade France. Much less impressive was the actual campaigning. The Duke of Burgundy proved himself to be unable or unwilling to supplement the English army with a sizeable Burgundian force. Faced with the likelihood of a prolonged and expensive campaign with little hope of success, Edward came to terms with the French king. At the Treaty of Picquigny in August 1475, Edward was to withdraw from France. His price was an immediate payment of 75,000 crowns, to be followed by a yearly pension of 50,000 crowns. The son of the French king (the Dauphin) was to marry Edward's daughter Elizabeth. A seven-year truce was to be observed between the two countries, and the treaty removed burdensome restrictions on English trade with France.

To what extent can the Treaty of Picquigny be seen as a success? If Edward IV had truly intended to become King of France in practice (he already claimed the title), then it was, of course, a disaster. It is, however, unlikely that Edward believed this to be a real possibility. A more meaningful aim was the recovery of the territories of Normandy and Gascony, lost by Henry VI. But the treaty did not give the king one extra handful of French soil. Nevertheless, the pension was well worth having. It made a very considerable contribution to Edward's solvency in the remaining years of his reign. So too did the trading arrangements, with the cloth trade of Devon and Bristol benefiting substantially. But what was really missing was the glory of conquest. To display personal valour was the mark of a true king, and to display it in France conferred yet more prestige. This is the greatest failing of the treaty. There is evidence to suggest that the English had to put up with taunts from the French and the Burgundians that their king was dishonoured, avaricious and a coward to boot. And there were certainly muted criticisms made of Edward in England itself. Perhaps we should conclude by saying that the outcome of Edward IV's great enterprise in France was a victory for realism. But this was its only victory.

Problems with France did not go away thanks to the Treaty of Picquigny. In 1477, Duke Charles the Bold of Burgundy was killed while besieging the town of Nancy. His daughter Mary was his heir, and Louis took the opportunity to invade the duchy. Edward was once more courted by both France and Burgundy. It may be that the fear of losing the pension hampered Edward's freedom of manoeuvre: only slowly and painfully did he move towards support of Maximilian of Austria, who had married Mary of Burgundy. In 1480, he pledged support - providing Maximilian would agree to pay the usual 50,000 crowns if France withdrew the pension. Before that support could translate into action, there was trouble on the Scottish border with raiding and pillaging of English territory in defiance of the truce between governments. It is possible that the trouble was at least encouraged by the French king. Edward's reaction was both heavy-handed and dilatory. He made extensive preparations (courtesy of taxes and benevolences) for an invasion, but failed to decide whether or not to lead his armies himself. By the time he had made the decision not to do so, the summer campaigning season of 1481 was over. Edward then decided to stir up trouble for the Scottish king by supporting the claims of the latter's brother, Alexander, Duke of Albany. In 1482, an English invasion under Richard of Gloucester capitalised on the unruly behaviour of the Scottish nobility. James III was captured and held in Edinburgh, which was taken by the English. Albany, however, reneged on the agreement with Edward in return for a restoration to his former positions and status. Gloucester - for reasons that are not at all clear - withdrew from his position of strength in Edinburgh. All the English gained was the recovery of Berwick-upon-Tweed. It is also unclear whether one should blame Gloucester or lack of direction from Edward himself. But, once again, money had been spent, opportunities lost and little gained.

Worse was to follow. By December 1482, Burgundy and France had come to terms at the Treaty of Arras: a treaty which pointedly excluded England. Maximilian, who had lost his wife in a riding accident, also lost considerable territory: and his baby daughter and heir, Margaret, was to marry the Dauphin. There was now no reason for Louis to continue to pay the pension to Edward, so he did not. Some contemporaries believed that Edward's anger at Arras and the loss of his pension hastened his premature death.

It is easy enough to argue that Edward IV's foreign policy was largely unsuccessful. He did at least achieve the recognition of his dynasty in Europe, but it hard to avoid the conclusion that foreign policy appears to have brought out the weaker side of his generally impressive character: a lack of a sense of direction, even an occasional laziness; and, towards the end of his reign, a pronounced avarice. The Treaty of Arras stands as an unfortunate monument to his failure. But, of course, treaties were frequently broken: had Edward lived longer, he could reasonably have expected the shifting world of alliances to have swung back in his favour. But it is true that he was generally out-manoeuvred by the spectacularly devious Louis XI, and that his embroilment in Scotland meant that he lacked the resources and will to intervene in French and Burgundian affairs when intervention was necessary. He really did not exploit the advantages of his position.

10 The Foreign Policy of Richard III

We have seen that England was in an unenviable and isolated diplomatic position by 1483. These difficulties were compounded by the usurpation. The doubtful (to use no stronger a word) circumstances of Gloucester's claim to and seizure of the throne had provided other European powers with a further weapon against England. They also elevated the status of the one real pretender to the throne, Henry Tudor, Earl of Richmond, who was living a precarious life of exile in Brittany.

In these circumstances, it says little for Richard III's statesmanship that he should fail to capitalise on the evident wish of the restored James III for peace with England. Richard chose to back Albany, who had fled to England after condemnation for treason in the Scottish Parliament of July 1483. Albany's English-sponsored raid into Scotland was a disaster, and he was forced to flee to France. Only at this point did Richard seem prepared to discuss peace with James III. In September 1484, a three-year truce was agreed (backed by a marriage treaty). This did not prevent James III from cementing the 'auld alliance' with France. A product of this relationship was the fact that a contingent of Scottish troops fought for Henry Tudor at Bosworth field.

Of greater immediate danger to Richard was the support Henry Tudor was receiving from the Duke of Brittany. Duke Francis's motives are simple enough to understand. He had a very valuable commodity in Henry Tudor: both France and England wanted him - for very different reasons, of course. This no doubt explains Francis's backing for the abortive invasion of October 1483 (see page 89). Richard's response was vigorous: a sensible policy of carrot and stick. The stick was the powerful English merchant fleet, which was to prey on Breton ships. The carrot, according to Polydore Vergil, was an offer to Duke Francis of the earldom of Richmond. There was also the possibility of an English military alliance against France, which was in some turmoil after the death of Louis XI. When Francis fell ill, his treasurer, Landais, determined to pack Henry Tudor off to England. Richard's policies therefore came within an ace of success, but the pretender to the English throne was tipped off and fled across the border to France.

Richard III is not to blame for this. However, the fact that the French assisted Henry Tudor's fateful invasion of August 1485 is, perhaps, indirectly the result of his policies. The French would interpret Richard's offer of support for Brittany as an action typical of the English enemy. Since he appeared to wish to destabilise France, why should he not be destabilised in return? Charles Ross feels that Richard could usefully have been more friendly towards France at this point: had he been so, then the French might have made little or no use of Henry Tudor. Possibly so: but Charles VIII's government would hardly have been impressed by proffered English friendship knowing full well that it was a direct result of Henry Tudor's presence in their kingdom. In any case, the years of suspicion of English intentions played their part. On the other hand, Richard seems never to have considered the possibility of using a warmer friendship with France to put pressure on Brittany for the return of his rival.

We might conclude, then, that Richard III's foreign policy was a conspicuous failure. He failed to prevent a foreign power from capitalising on a dangerous pretender by sponsoring an invasion of England. That failure led to his death. However, it has to be said that bad luck played its part. After all, Henry Tudor was very nearly handed over to Richard's tender mercies. Perhaps we should argue that, as far as we can tell from his brief reign and from his relations with France and Scotland, Richard III's approach to the fraught question of foreign policy was indeed cursed by misfortune, but was also rather inflexible and unsubtle.

11 The Yorkist Kings and Kingship

a) Edward IV

Edward IV may be said to have restored the authority of the monarchy following the disasters of the reign of Henry VI. His was a traditional kingship, capitalising on the equally traditional virtues of an effective king. He was prepared to supervise personally the workings of government. He remembered names and faces, and could deal on a personal level with all who had access to him. He had a considerable grasp of detail. He looked like a king. In all these facets of kingship, he was a marked contrast to his unfortunate predecessor.

However, there is a difference between a personal monarch and a monarch who relies heavily on his personality to govern. It was, perhaps, Edward's failing that he had the tendency to do the latter as well as be the former. In the crucial area of relations between magnates, he trusted to his own undeniable authority and charisma to control the corrosive jealousies of rival factions. But his early death exposed his lack of foresight. As we saw on page 84, he bequeathed a dangerous legacy to his sons, and they paid the price.

A king in Edward's mould was unlikely to be an innovator. He was, as we have seen, brought up to be heir to a dukedom, and can hardly have

been encouraged to plan for the changes he might make to the rôle of a
monarch when he grew up.

We have discovered that the New Monarchy concept has not proved
to be a helpful tool of analysis for the reign of Edward IV. Rather than
centralising power, he took the traditional course of relying on the
nobility as his agent in the localities. The great nobles retained their
independence and freedom of manoeuvre. It was Henry VII who
succeeded in making service at court, rather than extensive lands and
local authority, the benchmark of status for a noble. Edward IV made no
such attempt. Granted, he did choose to exploit the increasing
education of the lesser nobility by employing them in such rôles as
receivers: granted also that he elevated others to the dignity of magnate.
But this does not amount to a policy of supplanting the old nobility with
'new men' of markedly lower social status. Nor does it mean that the
power of the king increased at the expense of the nobility - another
supposed characteristic of New Monarchy.

There is little evidence that Edward IV attempted to promote a new
image of kingship. Henry VII employed the techniques of propaganda
by using a biographer (André) to argue that he was God's agent of
reconciliation between Yorkist and Lancastrian. Henry also sought to
make use of the alleged sanctity of Henry VI and the supposed descent
of the Tudors from the renowned King Arthur to increase the sense of
distance between king and (noble) subject. Edward, on the other hand,
had plenty of fellow-feeling for the class from which he had emerged. He
genuinely enjoyed the company of his nobility. And the nearest he came
to the regular use of propaganda was to make sure that royal
proclamations were read out in English in the larger centres of
population. It might also be argued that he used the pamphlet-style
Historie of the Arrivall in England of King Edward IV to claim that God
supported the recovery of his throne. But these few instances do not
amount to the projection of a new concept of monarchy.

When J.R. Green wrote *A Short History of the English People* in the
1870s, he not only argued that Edward IV was the founder of the New
Monarchy, but also that he was despotic: in fact, despotism, or the
exercise of an unconstrained, absolute authority, was supposed to be
part and parcel of New Monarchy itself. Was Edward IV a despot? Some
contemporary chroniclers clearly thought that he had that tendency and
intention. The judicial execution of his dangerous brother, the Duke of
Clarence, in 1478 was cited as an example. The Crowland chronicler
remarked that, after the death of Clarence, 'King Edward ... was now
persuaded that he could rule as he pleased throughout the whole
kingdom'. This anonymous chronicler was well-placed to judge, since,
as we recall, the internal evidence suggests that he was probably a royal
official. Also, Edward's use of benevolences - in effect, 'gifts' extracted
from the nobility, supposedly as an alternative to military service - might
be taken as further proof of creeping despotism. But the overall case is

not a strong one. The benevolences were never intended as a permanent system of taxation to sabotage the privileges of Parliament. They were responses to what Edward saw as his need in specific circumstances - namely, the threat of war. And it could be argued that Clarence brought about his own doom: indeed, Edward had shown considerable restraint considering his brother's behaviour. Unabashed by his earlier treason with Warwick, Clarence continued to be defiant, incapable of heeding some very clear warnings and a threat to the system of justice. After his wife had died in 1476, Clarence convinced himself that she had been poisoned. He blamed a former servant, dragged the unfortunate woman before justices of the peace and a jury, intimidated everyone in sight, and hanged her. If despotism implies a kind of tyrannical, arbitrary will. then one suspects that it was Clarence, rather than the king, who possessed it.

b) Richard III

Was Richard III a despotic king? It would be easy enough to write an entire book on the arguments on this issue, and a very interesting book it would be too. However, we must content ourselves here with a very brief examination of the question. In the full sense of the term, Richard III was not a despot. He preserved the systems of government and justice, called a parliament as the appropriate body to agree to legislation, and did not try to rule by the mere force of his will in defiance of all known forms. Indeed, his parliament made illegal the 'benevolences' beloved of Edward IV. Nevertheless, a case can still be made for Richard as a fundamentally despotic ruler.

We should remind ourselves first of all of Richard's behaviour in the months before his usurpation. The arrest and execution of Rivers, Grey, Vaughan (see page 81) and Hastings (see page 86) shows a spectacular disregard for even the semblance of legality. The four men were a threat, and were therefore removed permanently. The suggestion that Hastings was executed because he was involved in a plot against Richard is little more than wishful thinking on the past of Gloucester's more partisan defenders. Jeremy Potter's *Good King Richard* twists and turns in an attempt to play down the episode, commenting variously that there are no sure answers as to whether or not there was a plot, claiming that the execution of Hastings was 'uncharacteristic' of Richard (forgetting, presumably, the execution of Grey, Rivers and Vaughan) and then arguing on no evidence whatsoever that the the Duke of Buckingham 'may have been the instigator of the plot'. By far the most plausible explanation is that Hastings simply had to be removed, as he was the man most capable of rousing Edward IV's household men to defend the dead king's sons. And, as king, Richard showed scant respect for the law when granting away the land of rebels before they had been attainted by Act of Parliament. The most notorious act is the murder of Edward V and Richard of York: the 'Princes in the Tower'. Of course, one cannot obtain proof in the legal sense that the brothers died on Richard's orders. But a simple statement of the case suggests that by far the most likely culprit is the king. He certainly had the motive. While they were alive, they were a potential focus of plots against him. The 1483 rebellion probably started out as a movement to liberate the princes (see page 88). Second, he had the power and the opportunity. It is inconceivable that they could have been killed without his say so. The less sensible modern defenders of Richard have tried to wheel out Buckingham as the murderer, but there is no evidence to support such an unlikely assertion. Buckingham was doubtless an arrogant and ruthless man, but to suggest that he may have decided to have the princes killed without the express authority of the king defies belief. And finally, we have the simple fact that the princes disappeared from view in the summer of 1483. In the relatively small world of fifteenth- century England, a world of rumour, of gossip, and of intrigue, this could mean only one thing.

Richard's plantation of northerners to control the restive south of the country drew upon him the charge of despotic behaviour. The pro-southern Crowland chronicler complained bitterly of the 'tyranny' of the northerners. However, if we look at it another way, then it is clear that Richard III lacked the power to rule despotically even had he so wished. His reliance on his northern supporters is a testimony to the narrowness of his power-base. The Crowland chronicler reports that the king was obliged to state publicly that he had no intention to marry his niece Elizabeth (after the death of the queen) because his northerners feared her influence and threatened that they would turn against him.

Finally, we might consider whether Richard III's personality matches that of a despot or tyrant. But then it has to be said that there is a grave danger in historians attempting to analyse personality. Amateur psychology is of little help. Claiming to be able to see into someone's mind is worse. One can and should discuss motives, as long as that discussion is substantively corroborated by the character's actions. You might like to consider how far the sources below meet that criterion. Some are clearly distorted by using emotive (value-laden) language.

A From Jeremy Potter's *Good King Richard?* (1983):

He (Richard) seems to have been brave and resolute, honest and generous, benevolent and well-intentioned, patriotic and incor-ruptible, but of limited ability and intelligence and fatally impulsive. Pious, charitable and cultivated, he was a munificent patron of the church and of music and scholarship ... Loyal himself, he seems to have been unable to inspire loyalty in others ...

B From Polydore Vergil, whose work of history was written in the reigns of Henry VII and Henry VIII:

[Richard,] Duke of Gloucester ... thought of nothing but tyranny and cruelty ... He was little of stature, deformed of body, the one shoulder being higher than the other, a short and sour countenance, which seemed to savour of mischief, and utter evidently craft and deceit ... Truly, he had a sharp wit, provident and subtle, apt both to counterfeit and dissemble; his courage also high and fierce, which failed him not in the very death ...

C From M.A. Hicks, *Richard III as Duke of Gloucester: a Study in Character* (1986):

Richard's selfishness denotes both exceptional egotism and individualism. Whereas other magnates thought in the long term, seeking to maintain the family estates and to foster the interests of future generations of their dynasty, Richard gave priority to his own good, his immediate political needs and the eventual salvation of his soul.

D From Sir Thomas More, *History of King Richard the Third.* Written in the early part of Henry VIII's reign. More never completed it. Much of the information it contained derived from John Morton, the Bishop of Ely, who was an enemy of Richard III:

[Richard] was in wit and courage equal with either of [his brothers], in body and probity (uprightness) far under them both: little of stature, ill-featured of limbs, crook-backed ... He was malicious, wrathful, envious ... He was close and secret, a deep dissembler, lowly of countenance, arrogant of heart, outwardly companionable where he inwardly hated, not hesitating to kiss whom he thought to kill, pitiless and cruel, not for evil will always but oftener for ambition and either for the surety or increase of his position.

E From Charles Ross, *Richard III* (1981):

He [Richard] had two acknowledged bastards ... There are other indications that Richard was not the dour and earnest puritan which some of his modern admirers have proclaimed him to be. Richard was unfortunate in that he did not inherit the great height and powerful build of many of his Plantagenet predecessors ... There is no reliable evidence for the popular Tudor idea that he was hunchbacked.

Some historians have felt that Richard III's personality remains an enigma. Perhaps so, but we can at least use his recorded actions to make some tentative suggestions. He appears to have been uncommonly ruthless in an age where ruthlessness was common, and startlingly

Portrait of Richard III, c. 1590, artist unknown

Portrait of Richard III ('Broken Sword'), painted between 1572-7, artist unknown

Portrait of Richard III; a copy of an original painted during Richard's lifetime (the copy was painted about 1513)

ambitious in an age when ambition rarely startled. This was an explosive combination. His reign was too short to allow the fall-out from usurpation and execution to settle. His positive qualities of courage, a certain piety and an interest in justice are all but buried beneath the débris.

12 Conclusion

What, then, are the main characteristics of Yorkist monarchy? Perhaps we should remind ourselves that both Edward IV and Richard III were born and brought up as dukes rather than kings. They were good at the things effective dukes were good at: the management of resources, intervening personally when needed, watching over the accounts, making sure that law and order neither broke down nor interfered with the position of the nobility. This meant that they stood for a traditional and reinvigorated kingship, which benefited from their sheer capacity for hard work (when they deemed it necessary), a fund of energy and a resolute courage.

Edward IV's reign put an end to the conflict of Henry VI's time and established a level of law and order which at least prevented large-scale riot and civil strife. The limitations of that style of kingship must, however, be stressed. The king's policies - particularly in the final years of his reign - were intended to increase his personal wealth, and drew upon him the exaggerated criticism of the Crowland chronicler, who, as we have seen, felt that the Yorkist king tended towards despotism. But sufficient of his innate generosity remained to blunt the impact of his greedier latter days. So too did his love of luxurious living and sensuality. In any case, the king lacked the sustained ruthlessness and vision of the true despot. He relied on the impact of his impressive personality to deal with the tensions among his magnates, but failed to plan for the future. His impulsiveness - the Woodville marriage, for instance - was not a fatal flaw, but its consequences were exacerbated by an unwillingness or inability to tackle problems at their root. The potentially dangerous rivalries between the Woodvilles and the Gloucester-Hastings factions were controlled but never really addressed by the king. Had he lived another five years, then these failings might well have been of little consequence. But Edward IV's over-confidence in his personal authority and ready charm was matched by a similar over-confidence in the ability of his impressive constitution to withstand his gargantuan over-eating and indulgence. Both were misplaced.

The reign of Richard III was characterised both by continuity and by discontinuity. There is continuity in financial administration through the chamber system of finance and through the attempt to exploit feudal revenues. The discontinuity was not of Richard's choice. He was unable to retain the loyalty of a considerable number of his brother's household men, with the result that he was forced to rely increasingly on the northerners he could trust. Edward IV's power-base was not exactly narrow, but it was dominated to an unhealthy extent by a small number of great magnate factions. Richard's power-base was significantly smaller.

There are some signs that Richard III would have made an effective king given time. His interest in justice for all may have been more than pious words, and he had sufficient vision to set up the Council of the North as an alternative to relying upon magnates (like the Earl of Northumberland) whom he was not sure he could trust. But the circumstances of his usurpation and the likely murder of the Princes in the Tower compromised his régime: he inspired little trust himself. In some ways, he seems like a rather bad caricature of his eldest brother: more ruthless, more impulsive but, in the end, less impressive.

The New Monarchy concept has not been considered to be an appropriate label to attach to Yorkist monarchy. There is little evidence of a deliberate policy of centralisation, of administrative innovation or of a major shift in power away from the nobility. Nor were the Yorkists presenting a new image of kingship. It is often argued that Henry VII built upon the foundations laid by the Yorkists to create something close to a New Monarchy. Perhaps so: but there is something of an irony if the one enduring legacy of Yorkist rule was to provide the basis for the success of the usurper who destroyed their dynasty.

Making notes on *'The Government of Edward IV and Richard III'*

Although this chapter is self-contained, it would be helpful to remember that previous chapters have also shown Yorkist government in action. It is not essential, although it might be helpful, to try to cross-reference when making notes, but you should definitely be prepared to use previous information as examples in essays.

1.   Introduction. Notes not needed.

2.   New Monarchy. What are the main characteristics of New Monarchy theory? What are the potential dangers of using a 'model' like New Monarchy?

3.   Edward IV, Richard III and the Political Nation

3.1   How far did Edward IV treat the nobility in the traditional manner?

3.2   What policy did Richard III adopt towards the nobility? What were his motives?

3.3   Why did Richard III set up the Council of the North? Is it to be seen as an example of New Monarchy in action?

3.4   What conclusions can we come to on the relevance of the New Monarchy concept to the Yorkists' relations with the nobility?

4.   Law and Order under Edward IV

4.1   Retaining. What steps did Edward IV take on retaining? Why did he fail to curb it?

4.2   Justice. How innovative and successful was Edward IV in providing justice?

5.   Law and Order under Richard III

5.1   What evidence is there that Richard was concerned to promote justice for all? How far do his actions back up his words?

5.2   How far does the New Monarchy model apply to the Yorkist kings and Justice?

6.   The Revenue of the King. Describe the medieval king's revenue system.

7.   The Finances of the Yorkist kings

7.1   The Collection of Revenue: Exchequer *versus* Chamber. Why, and with what effect, did Edward IV adopt a chamber system of finance?

7.2   How far does the chamber system of finance fit the New Monarchy model?

7.3   The Crown becomes solvent. How had the king succeeded in becoming solvent?

7.4   Richard III and Finance. Compare Richard's financial policies with those of Edward IV.

8.   Yorkist Foreign Policy - an Introduction

8.1   What were the general aims of English foreign policy, and how far did these reflect the power of the king over foreign policy?

8.2   What were the specific aims of the Yorkist kings?

9.   The Foreign Policy of Edward IV

9.1   In what ways might we consider Edward's foreign policy to be largely successful by 1464?

9.2   What factors led Louis XI to back the Lancastrian invasion of 1470?

9.3   The Treaty of Picquigny, 1475. How far can this treaty be seen as a success for Edward?

9.4   Is it fair to consider Edward's foreign policy in the final years of his reign as a failure?

10.   The Foreign Policy of Richard III. Why might that policy be considered an unmitigated failure? What factors led to its failure?

11.   The Yorkist Kings and Kingship

11.1 Edward IV. What conclusions can we come to on the applicability of the New Monarchy concept to the goevrnment of Edward IV?

11.2 How despotic was Edward IV?

11.3 Richard III. How despotic was the behaviour of Richard III? What conclusions can we come to on his personality?

12.   Conclusion. What are the main characteristics of Yorkist monarchy?

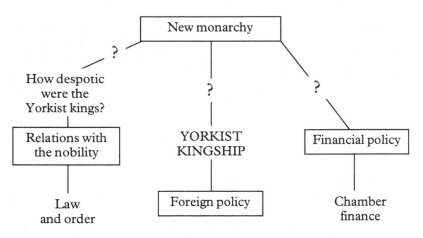

Summary - The Government of Edward IV and Richard III

Answering essay questions on *'The Government of Edward IV and Richard III'*

It is certainly possible that examiners might ask a question comparing the Yorkist kings to Henry VII. Although there have been a number of comparisons made with Henry VII, this book has not sought to equip you to answer such a wide-ranging question. It has equipped you to answer the relatively familiar comparison question on Edward IV and Richard III. Less likely is the same type comparing Henry VI and the Yorkists, if only because most syllabuses start c.1450 - by which time Henry VI had been ruling (for want of a better word) for over a decade.

Questions purely on Edward IV are common. Less so are questions purely on Richard III: hardly surprising, given the brevity of his reign. The questions that do appear sometimes involve commenting on the view that Richard was a tyrant or despot. In fact, it is essential that you remind yourself of the meaning of those two words. And, while we are on the subject of concepts, make sure you are familiar with New Monarchy. Here are some typical questions.

1 How successful were the Yorkist kings in establishing good order?
2 What was novel and what was traditional in Yorkist kingship?
3 'More of a duke than a king'. Is this a fair assessment of Edward IV?
4 'Yorkist monarchy stopped short of despotism purely because of the personal weaknesses of its kings.' How far is this an accurate view of the reigns of Edward IV and Richard III?
5 'Edward IV reinvigorated traditional kingship'. How far do you accept this view?

Think about the following issues. a) In which of these questions might you wish to discuss New Monarchy? b) Try to put the questions in order of difficulty, and explain your response. c) How would you structure an analytical essay on government? You might like to use the structure of this chapter, which divides up the material into relations with the political nation, law and order, finance and foreign policy.

Source-based questions on *'The Government of Edward IV and Richard III'*

1 The Personality of Richard III
Study the extracts on pages 142-3 and the illustrations on pages 144 and 145. Answer the following questions.
a) Which portrait most clearly matches the attitude towards Richard expressed by More in source D? Explain your answer. (3 marks)
b) How might one explain the differences between the portraits? (4 marks)
c) What value do such portraits have for the historian studying the period of the Wars of the Roses? (5 marks)
d) Some contemporary or near contemporary historians are often dismissed as worthless and inaccurate by modern defenders of Richard III. Carefully read sources B and D, and consider how far this attitude appears to be justified. (5 marks)
e) Which of the three modern historians do you consider to be least accurate in their analyses of Richard III? Explain the reasons for your choice by referring to sources A, C and E. What other information, if any, would you need before you could be sure of your answer? (8 marks)

CHAPTER 7

Conclusion

1 Writing Conclusions

In *Elizabeth I: Religion and Foreign Affairs* (in this series), I made the non-controversial suggestion that few students like writing conclusions to essays. I also suggested how conclusions might be approached, and then attempted to base my own conclusion on that advice. I intend to do exactly the same for *The Wars of the Roses and the Yorkist Kings,* and those readers who go on to use *Elizabeth I* must forgive the apparent repetition. Look on it as helpful consistency.

Conclusions should do a number of things. First, they should provide a brief but vivid summary of the main arguments. Second, they should place the topics and discussions in a wider context. Third, if appropriate, they should identify where conclusions have to be tentative due to the nature of the evidence.

2 The Causes of the Wars of the Roses

The argument of Chapters 3 and 4 led us to reject as superficial the view that the conflicts known as the Wars of the Roses had the same cause. We should remind ourselves that there were - arguably - four sets of conflicts. The outbreak of the Wars in 1459 terminated in the usurpation of Edward IV in 1461. In 1469 and 1470, Edward was faced with the two Warwick rebellions, and recovered his throne in 1471. The third conflict was that surrounding the usurpation of Richard III in 1483: his brief reign encompasses further conflict in the rebellion of 1483 and terminated in the king's death in battle against Henry Tudor in 1485. The final conflicts of the Wars of the Roses featured the pretenders Simnel and Warbeck: the more serious threat (from Simnel) ended in 1487 at the battle of Stoke.

The outbreak of the Wars of the Roses stemmed from the attempt by Richard, Duke of York to impose himself by force on the government of Henry VI: in other words, to assume what he saw as his rightful place in the king's counsels. Without that place, he could see no safety for himself or his family. This was dangerous enough, but he increased the stakes by attempting to seize the throne as the ultimate source of security. We argued that this situation developed largely due to the spectacular incompetence of Henry VI. This was not to deny that there were longer-term problems within that violent society. Any king of the time had to recognise that the power of the magnate class had been growing substantially, and that the great nobles had the opportunities *via* bastard feudalism to acquire a large and potentially dangerous armed following. But kings were there to deal with such problems. In any case, a powerful nobility was a source of strength to an effective king. An enfeebled nobility meant an enfeebled king. But Henry VI appeared to have a Midas touch in reverse. Everything that was valuable crumbled in his hands. A king should increase his strength by balancing factions: he let them dominate him. The son of a great warrior-king should show the same lust for glory and booty: but Normandy and Gascony slipped from his nerveless fingers. His powers of patronage should have bound his nobles to him: instead, his prodigality led to a dangerous distribution of crown lands which sabotaged his power and provoked quarrels.

However, it was the emergence of Queen Margaret of Anjou as the aggressive defender of her young son Edward which pushed Richard of York over the brink. Rightly convinced that the queen wanted to destroy him and his family completely, he made his bid for the throne. This bid led to his death, but also, in the end, to the crowning of his son as Edward IV.

Is this a case of conflict caused by an over-mighty noble? If one were to define an over-mighty noble as one who seeks to overthrow the position and authority of the king, then, on one level, York is an over-mighty noble. But Richard of York did not seek the throne because he was over-mighty: nor did he have a vested interest in destabilising the monarchy. York's problems arose because the monarchy destabilised itself. And, in so doing, it threatened him with destruction.

If we now examine the second set of conflicts - the rebellions of Warwick in Edward IV's reign - then we need to answer the same question: was Warwick the Kingmaker an over-mighty noble? On the face of it, he fits the bill perfectly. He did indeed threaten the power and authority of the king. After all, his rebellions were caused largely by his desire to dominate Edward IV. And he certainly started the reign as an over-mighty subject, thanks to the fact that he had been the chief supporter of Edward's usurpation. Furthermore, it could be argued that he rebelled against the king because he felt his position was under threat. This was true, in so far as Edward was building up men such as Herbert and Hastings to counterbalance Warwick. But Edward was not seeking to destroy Warwick, or even to reduce him to the level of other magnates. He continued to be generous to the earl, but quite rightly recognised that to have a one-man power-base was to have no power-base at all. But Warwick simply could not - or would not - see it that way. He was incapable of accepting that his dominant position could not last. He could not cope with the realisation that, although he might retain a privileged place among the nobility, a good king could not allow him the vice-regal status he craved. A more astute and a more politically adept man might have accepted that a position won through war was inappropriate to peace. But not Warwick. The genuine difficulties of his position were inflamed by his greed, egocentricity and fundamental unreasonableness. His treason was caused directly by his own cravings for a power that would have destabilised the country as surely as his rebellions did. And so, Warwick was over-mighty because of the special circumstances of Edward's usurpation: but that was not enough to cause his rebellion directly. His own special brand of overweening arrogance and lack of political sense did that.

If we continue the theme of the over-mighty noble, do Edward IV's brothers fit the bill? We can agree that Clarence does, as his power and ambition certainly represented a threat to the king. Richard of Gloucester, however, was no threat to Edward IV. But he certainly was to the uncrowned Edward V.

Richard of Gloucester's usurpation was not directly caused by Edward IV's failure to reconcile differences between the Woodvilles and the other magnate factions, although that failure was a contributory factor. We accepted that Gloucester would fear that the young Edward V might avenge his Woodville relatives once his minority was over. But fear of possible consequences is one thing and usurpation quite another. Hastings had no love for the Woodvilles and had made that perfectly clear, but he never aspired to the downfall of Edward IV's sons. Gloucester was sufficiently self-obsessed and sufficiently ruthless to seek the throne. In the end, we should accept that he did so because he craved the power of kingship and - perhaps - was too much the slave of his own impulses. There was no justification in any legal sense for his seizure of the throne. The depths to which he would stoop in the quest for power are revealed in the atrocious allegation (if Mancini is to be believed) that his own mother had committed adultery in conceiving Edward IV. The charge of over-mighty noble might be laid on the Richard of Gloucester of Edward V's reign, and that charge would stick.

Can the same charge be laid against the Duke of Buckingham? Once again, he does seem to meet the criteria. He was powerful, and he did threaten the king. His motives for rebelling might be obscure, but it is reasonable to assume that he felt he was striving to safeguard an unusually strong position.

It is impossible to see Henry Tudor as an over-mighty noble. He relied on the support of others, rather than on his own power. His success was the result of a number of factors which had little to do with that power (or lack of it). In the first place, a significant number of Edward's household men bitterly resented the usurpation and the disappearance of the young princes. This explains why Richard III was obliged to rely on a small group of nobles whom he could trust and a smaller group of magnates whose trustworthiness was less certain. He failed to prevent Henry Tudor from receiving help from France in his invasion of 1485, but Tudor's success on the battlefield owed more to Richard's impulsiveness than to the timely support of the shifty Stanleys.

What conclusions, then, can we come to on the significance of the so-called 'over-mighty nobility'? First, it is quite wrong to see this nobility as the dominant factor in causing the Wars. As we have seen, the outbreak was largely due to the deficiencies of the monarch. Second, it must be stressed that the nobility was not typically over-mighty. The position of Warwick and Buckingham was mighty enough, but was the product of the special circumstances of a usurpation. And, even then, there was needed the added ingredient of power-lust and ruthlessness that stemmed from a noble's personality rather than his status. Warwick had it, and so did Richard of Gloucester. Buckingham probably did, but we are less clear on the motives of his rebellion.

And finally, we can attribute the conflicts in Henry VII's reign to a relatively simple cause. Some Yorkists were unwilling to come to terms with the new régime, and therefore sought a Yorkist monarch. Dynastic pride played a part, no doubt, but so did resentment at loss of position and power. Some were more than happy to accept the false pretenders Simnel and Warbeck for the simple reason that they would be easier to manipulate.

So: the causes of the various conflicts known collectively as the Wars of the Roses were not identical. It is hardly surprising that there were common features, but the temptation to claim that they were all the result of the same cause should be resisted. It is also tempting to argue that they were self-perpetuating in the sense that nobles began to see rebellion less as a last resort and more as a normal way of achieving what they wanted. This view is superficially attractive, but it would not do to overstress it. After all, both Edward IV and Henry VII were able to impose relative stability and calm after the storms.

3 The Impact of the Wars of the Roses

I thoroughly enjoyed writing the 'Blood and Gore' section in Chapter 1, where the reader was invited to dwell on the traditional view of the blood-soaked political landscape of England. I did so reasonably safe in the knowledge - or the belief - that it was a gross exaggeration. This is not to claim that the country was a 'merrie England' of peaceful peasants and bustling towns with the occasional and rather picturesque battle to enliven the dull routine of the workaday world. English society was marked by an undercurrent of violence and disorder and, in the short term, the Wars made it far worse. There is nothing charming or picturesque about the casualty figures of the battle of Towton, or about the assassination of rivals, or about the judicial and non-judicial murders of nephews and brothers. But to argue that the Wars came close to destroying the economic life of the country, or left devastated villages in their wake, or irreparably damaged the relationship between noble and monarch, is simply inaccurate. A change in the relationship between monarch and noble is detectable in the reign of Henry VII, but the increased control over the nobility which this king secured reflected his particular skills and policies rather than the actual legacy of the Wars of the Roses. But they did make excellent propaganda for the Tudors. Better a strong king than chaos: better to accept the will of the monarch than to suffer the edge of a sword. As people forgot what the conflicts were really like, an inaccurate portrayal of the Wars of the Roses became more and more useful to the Tudor kings.

This is not to say that the evidence which leads us to these conclusions is easy to use. Chroniclers were notoriously unreliable when counting corpses, and the actual length, severity of and participation in campaigns remain issues surrounded with uncertainty. Evidence from domestic and religious architecture was not in itself convincing proof of the relative stability and prosperity of the country, but it did prove to be useful as corroboration.

4 The Wars of the Roses in a European Context

Why seek to put the Wars into this wider context? There are two main reasons. First, as was suggested on page 133, England was not an island - it was only half of one. Nor was it immune to the influence of the rest of Europe. How could it be when its kings claimed also to be Kings of France? How could it be, when English monarchs retained a foothold in France in the shape of Calais, itself a remnant of far greater possessions, so recently lost? And second, comparison is particularly useful. When Commynes argued that England was a remarkably peaceful country (see page 115), he did so by comparing it with its European neighbours.

From Scotland to France and to the kingdoms of Spain, civil war was a common experience. As A.J. Pollard had pointed out, the stability of these monarchies - like that of England - rested on the abilities of individual kings. There are other tempting similarities. Successful monarchs, like Henry Tudor and like Ferdinand of Aragon and his wife Isabella of Castille, tended to over-emphasise the chaos of past civil war to encourage support for their own régimes. Enrico IV of Castille (half-brother of Isabella) had failings all too reminiscent of Henry VI, and was villified by his successor in much the same way as Richard III was villified by Henry VII. And the authority of European monarchs appears to have been enhanced by the civil wars.

However, significant as these similarities might be, it is easy to overstate them. The authority of the kings of France and Scotland over their respective kingdoms was markedly less than that of the English king over England. The Scottish nobles had considerably greater autonomy than their English counterparts, and the activities of the Dukes of Burgundy frequently threatened the very throne of France. As with many such generalisations, the idea of a crisis throughout fifteenth-century Europe effectively obscures such differences. In any case, one has to question what a generalisation of this type actually explains. It may be significant that A.J. Pollard's discussion of these issues leads to little by way of an explanation of why civil war should permeate Europe. There is a further danger. We have seen that the causes of the conflicts in England were by no means consistent: any attempt to relate them to conflicts elsewhere in Europe carries with it the danger that we will minimise this diversity in the name of broad and, perhaps, increasingly meaningless analogies.

5 The Yorkist Kings

It was suggested on page 1 that, when Henry V died, his early death both sealed and magnified his fame as the great warrior king. The early deaths of Edward IV and Richard III - the last of the Plantagenet kings of England - sealed the downfall of their dynasty. But it would be most unfair to write them off as failures. Without being major innovators - and certainly not New Monarchs in the historiographical sense - they successfully transcended their lack of training in the kingly art and proved to be effective kings in the traditional mould. Despite his failings, Edward IV succeeded in restoring the prestige and enhanced the wealth of the monarchy. His nobility respected him and was aware that he was not to be crossed with impunity. He curbed the most flagrant violations of law and order. He showed an intelligent interest in commerce and, although his foreign policy was compromised near the end of his reign, he had certainly established his dynasty on the European stage. Richard III shared many of his brother's qualities and had the good sense to appreciate the value of continuity, even though his usurpation was the denial of it. He retained the effective system of chamber finance and spoke well about justice: but he could not retain the support of many of his brother's household men and could get few to speak well of him. His death at Bosworth field was not the inevitable result of lack of support, but the mistaken, if courageous, impulse to meet his adversary Henry Tudor at the point of a sword. If it had not been for this rush of blood he might have won the battle of Bosworth, or at least survived to fight another day. His régime was compromised by the circumstances of his seizure of the throne and the disappearance of his nephews, but it is possible that, given luck and time, it could have stabilised.

6 The Significance of 1485

The older historiographical tradition magnified the importance of the accession of Henry VII as if it marked the end of the so-called Middle Ages and the start of the modern or early modern age. More recent orthodoxy has refuted this interpretation. But it has to be said that the reign of Henry VII was, in some ways, a crucial break with the past. As has been suggested, there is a significant change in the relationship between king and nobility. This issue is discussed in greater detail in Caroline Rogers' *Henry VII* in the *Access to History* series. While it could hardly be argued that Henry attempted to sabotage the power of the nobility, he most certainly sought to control that power in the interests of the crown. A great noble was great because he had a place of importance at court, and not because he ruled a vast inheritance virtually independent of the king.

7 A Few Words to the Reader

On page 1, it was accepted that for some readers - particularly student readers - this book may well represent their first real acquaintance with late medieval history. Hopefully, some of the real remoteness, and, dare it be said, the romance, of the period will have been recognised but understood on its own terms. Historians are rightly suspicious of sentimental views of history, but they would be wrong to forget that there is an intrinsic interest in ways of life and attitudes remote from one's own.

Chronological Table

1421   Birth of Henry VI
1422   Death of Henry V
1436   Richard of York Lieutenant-General in France
1437   End of Henry VI's minority
1440-5   Richard of York's second period as Lieutenant-General
1443   John Beaufort, Duke of Somerset, appointed Captain-General of France
1444   Truce of Tours with France. Betrothal of Henry VI and Margaret of Anjou
1445   Marriage of Henry VI and Margaret of Anjou
1447   Edmund Beaufort, Duke of Somerset, replaced York. York appointed Lieutenant of Ireland
1450   Loss of Normandy. Impeachment, banishment and murder of Suffolk. Cade rebellion. York returned from Ireland
1453   Talbot killed at Castillon. Gascony lost. Henry VI insane. Birth of Henry VI's son, Edward
1454   York appointed Protector
1455   Henry VI recovered. 1st Battle of St Albans - death of Somerset and Northumberland. Henry VI insane again. York's second protectorate
1456   Henry VI recovered. York relieved of Protectorate
1459   York fled to Ireland. Parliament of the Devils
1460   Battle of Northampton. York claimed throne. Act of Accord. Battle of Wakefield (Sandal) - death of York
1461   2nd Battle of St Albans. Edward IV proclaimed king in London. Battle of Towton
1462   Abortive landing of Margaret of Anjou in Northumberland.
1464   Somerset defected: Lancastrian rising in the north. Edward IV married Elizabeth Woodville
1465   Capture of Henry VI
1468   Marriage of Charles the Bold of Burgundy with Margaret of York
1469   Rebellion of Robin of Redesdale. Marriage of Clarence and Isabel Neville. First Warwick rebellion. Battle of Edgecote - Edward IV captured
1470   Warwick's second rebellion. Flight of Clarence and Warwick. Reconciliation of Warwick and Margaret of Anjou. Lancastrians landed at Dartmouth and Plymouth. Edward IV fled to Burgundy. Readeption of Henry VI

1471   Return of Edward IV. Warwick killed at Battle of Barnet. Battle
       of Tewkesbury: Prince Edward killed. Henry VI murdered in
       Tower of London
1474   Treaty of London
1475   Edward IV invaded France. Treaty of Picquigny
1478   Death of Clarence
1483   Death of Edward IV. Edward V proclaimed king. Intercepted
       by Gloucester at Stony Stratford. Execution of Hastings.
       Gloucester claimed the throne as Richard III. Rebellion
       involving Buckingham. Death of Buckingham
1484   Death of Richard III's son and heir (Edward)
1485   Landing of Henry Tudor, Earl of Richmond, at Milford Haven.
       Battle of Bosworth field. Death of Richard III. Henry VII king
1486   Henry VII married Elizabeth of York
1487   Battle of Stoke (Lambert Simnel)
1491   Perkin Warbeck in Ireland
1497   Capture of Warbeck in Cornwall
1509   Death of Henry VII

Further Reading

1 Surveys

There are a number of books which cover similar ground to *The Wars of the Roses and the Yorkist Kings*. A brief but helpful analysis is provided by **David R. Cook,** *Lancastrians and Yorkists: The Wars of the Roses* (Longman, 1984).

A more complex but still relatively short book is **A.J. Pollard,** *The Wars of the Roses* (Macmillan, 1988). You are likely to find this most useful once you have built up a sound understanding of the major themes. However, it has little on Yorkist government.

A book with massive extracts from documents linked by the briefest of narratives is **J.R. Lander,** *The Wars of the Roses* (Alan Sutton, 1990).

For contrasting views of the impact of the Wars of the Roses, consult **Anthony Goodman,** *The Wars of the Roses: Military Activity and English Society, 1452-97* (Routledge and Kegan Paul, 1981), and **John Gillingham,** *The Wars of the Roses: Peace and Conflict in Fifteenth-Century England* (Weidenfeld and Nicolson, 1981). Gillingham's introduction is wonderfully lively. He perhaps underestimates the effect of the Wars, whereas Goodman paints a much more sombre picture. An older, but arguably more balanced, book on the same theme is **Charles Ross,** *The Wars of the Roses: a Concise History* (Thames and Hudson, 1976).

2 Biographies

There are some superb biographies in this period. In particular, I can strongly recommend:

Bertram Wolffe, *Henry VI* (Methuen, 1981); **Charles Ross,** *Edward IV* (Methuen, 1974); **Charles Ross,** *Richard III* (Methuen, 1981).

These are all reasonably weighty tomes, so you might prefer to dip into them rather than to read them from cover to cover. But the more of them you can manage the better, for they really are authoritative. Ross is cool and judicious: Wolffe is livelier and inclined to savage Henry VI somewhat. If you develop a particular interest in that unfortunate king, you might like to compare Wolffe with:

R.A. Griffiths, *The Reign of King Henry VI* (Ernest Benn, 1981).

3 Primary sources

The standard (and massive) compilation of sources covering most aspects of life in fifteenth-century England is **A.R. Myers (ed.),**

English Historical Documents, IV, 1327-1485 (1969).

An excellent (and conveniently-sized) compilation of sources for the end of Edward IV's reign and that of Richard III is **Keith Dockray,** *Richard III: a Reader in History* (Alan Sutton, 1988). Dockray has also written a useful introduction to *Three Chronicles of the Reign of Edward IV* (Alan Sutton, 1988). For those who develop an obsession with Richard III, Dockray's reader can be supplemented by the many sources woven into the narrative of **P.W. Hammond and A.F. Sutton,** *Richard III: The Road to Bosworth Field* (Constable, 1985).

Acknowledgements

The publishers would like to thank the following for permission to reproduce material in this volume:

Alan Sutton Publishing for extracts from *The Wars of the Roses,* J.R. Lander, (1990); Borthwick Papers no. 70 *Richard III as Duke of Gloucester: A Study in Character,* Professor M.A. Hicks (1986); Constable Publishers for extracts from *Richard III: The Road to Bosworth Field,* P.W. Hammond and Anne F. Sutton, (1985) and extracts from *Good King Richard?,* J. Potter, (1983); The Folio Society for extracts from *Richard III: The Great Debate,* P. Kendall ed., (1965); Methuen London for extracts from *Richard III,* C. Ross, (1981), and *1066 and All That,* W.C. Sellar and R.J. Yeatman, (1930); by permission of Oxford University Press, extracts from *Paston Letters and Papers of the Fifteenth Century part 1,* N. Davis ed., (1971) and *The Paston Letters,* N. Davis ed., (1983).

Every effort has been made to trace and acknowledge ownership of copyright. The publishers will be glad to make suitable arrangements with any copyright holders whom it has not been able to contact.

Index